John Barnes + Diana Lentzer.

# Growing Food
# In the High Desert Country

# Growing Food
# In the High Desert Country

*By*
*Julie Behrend Weinberg*

*Sunstone Press*
*Santa Fe, New Mexico*

Copyright © 1985 by Julie Behrend Weinberg

All Rights Reserved.
No part of this book may be reproduced in any form or by any electronic
or mechanical means including information storage and retrieval systems,
without permission in writing from the publisher,
except by a reviewer who may quote brief passages in a review.

First Edition

Printed in the United States of America

Library of Congress Cataloging in Publication Data:

Weinberg, Julie Behrend, 1957-
    Growing food in the high desert country.

    Bibliography: p. 93
    Includes index.
    1. Vegetable gardening--Southwest, New. 2. Fruit-
culture--Southwest, New. 3. Desert gardening--Southwest,
New.    I. Title.
SB321.W44    1985        635'.0970        85-2682
ISBN: 0-86534-066-8

Published in 1985 by SUNSTONE PRESS
                Post Office Box 2321
                Santa Fe, NM 87504-2321 / USA

# CONTENTS

*Acknowledgement*

I want to thank my husband, Richard Y. Weinberg; my
parents, Dean and Sandra Behrend; and my grandparents,
Irving and Ceil Klein for the love and support that helped
to make this book a reality.

*Dedication*

This book is dedicated to the memory of my grandparents,
Morris and Molly Behrend.

# INTRODUCTION

When it was first suggested that I write this book, I immediately objected. What the world didn't need, I felt was another gardening book. But as I thought about it, I realized that the Southwest, especially the high desert country, has long been ignored by most of the horticultural community. Frequently envisioned as an endless desert where nothing but cacti grow, little has been written to help the high desert dweller cope with the problems of raising plants in a dry land.

The first vegetable garden I attempted in the Southwest was situated on the eastern slopes of the Sandia Mountains, the range that lies just east of Albuquerque, New Mexico. I was an "eastern" gardener then and I was surprised, frustrated and dismayed that my nifty, East Coast gardening techniques proved to be unsuitable for the conditions in the high desert. Thus began my journey into the world of high desert gardening, and though I'm sure that I'll learn a lot more before the journey is finished, over the years I've come up with a basic approach that works within the limits of this beautiful but austere area.

The "high desert country" that this book refers to is generally above 5500 feet and receives about 12 inches of rain annually. In general, if the locale has hot but not blistering summer days (mean highs in the 80s), cool summer nights (lows ranging from 50 to 65 degrees F.), a lot of wind, a dry spring and a monsoon season sometime between July and September, then this book is suited to that area. I also feel that this book is relevant for areas of the high desert that receive higher amounts of precipitation, such as the Flagstaff, Arizona area and the high mountain valleys. And for those hardy souls living in the highest elevations of the Sonoran Desert in southern Arizona, the techniques presented on the following pages will also work in your area, taking into account the slightly different climate and growing season. Even the Central Rio Grande Valley gardener who has the benefits of more moderate winter temperatures and warm summer nights can take advantage of many of the ideas and techniques presented in this book.

This book is not meant to be an exhaustive text about gardening. There are a number of excellent gardening books that provide lots of general information that all gardeners need to know. Unfortunately, the big volumes rarely include a section about gardening in the desert, let alone the high desert. Beginning high desert gardeners often run into problems trying to follow the advice of most general gardening books. So this book is designed to supplement and complement the general gardening volumes, providing information and ideas that will make high desert gardening a successful endeavor for everyone.

I have chosen to concentrate on food gardening for two basic reasons. The first is that vegetable gardening and orcharding are pleasant pastimes and extremely useful. While flower gardens and ornamental trees beautify our homes, which is very important, vegetable gardens and fruit trees fill our freezers and pantries. With high prices and low quality at the produce counter, not to mention the lack of variety, a vegetable garden and/or an orchard is a sane way to provide our families with good and varied food at economy prices.

The harvest provides a bonus above and beyond filling our stomachs: a feeling of satisfaction and freedom. That green patch in the yard or in the community garden will come to represent liberation from the pesticide-laden valleys of California, from the wage demands of truck drivers, and the vagaries of the marketplace.

While I focus on food gardening, those readers who also want to grow flowers and ornamental trees and shrubs (and I encourage everyone to do so) can find the basic information provided in this book useful. Simply learn what each plant demands in the way of nutrients, environment and care, and then apply the principles spelled out in the following chapters. Listings of drought-tolerant ornamental perennials, shrubs, and trees are provided at the end of the book.

The second reason I wrote this book was to encourage people to garden and thus get to know and respect the high desert more intimately. Here in the high desert, a person is confronted by its stark beauty every time he or she steps outside, yet so few of us are really in tune with this beauty. What better way to learn about the rhythms of the high desert and this planet than to put your hands in its soil and your face in its sun?

Stand in the first summer rain. Fill your lungs with the ozone-flavored air that follows a thunderstorm. Get to know the four basic elements — soil, sun, water and air — that nourish all livings things on Earth. From this intimate knowledge comes a respect and concern for the quality of the environmnent and the quality of life, today and in the future.

A garden always improves the quality of life, and gardening with respect for the fragile high desert ecosystem helps to preserve the good quality of life that is found here. In this day and age, when the hustle and bustle of modern life seems to be invading the traditionally slower-paced towns of the high desert, the human spirit needs a place to go and a job to do that is at once relaxing and creative. A vegetable garden, no matter what size it is, is that place and that job. It will reward you every season of the year.

# THE HIGH DESERT'S TROUBLESOME TRIO: CLIMATE, WATER SUPPLY AND SOIL   I

Many of the world's earliest civilizations developed in the fertile river valleys of arid lands. It is widely thought that agriculture, the base upon which civilization grew, was first practiced in the valleys of the Tigris and the Euphrates rivers. These rivers flow through a very arid land: present-day Iraq.

The Anasazi Indians of the high desert developed their civilizations in the river valleys of what is today called northern New Mexico, northern Arizona, southern Colorado and southern Utah. Given the choice, they could hardly have selected a more difficult climate to farm in all of the temperate world. But the choice was not theirs to make, and they struggled to feed themselves in a land of perpetual drought, undependable ground water supplies and poor soil. Today, many of the Anasazi's descendants still farm the high desert, battling the ancient foes with modern tools.

It is certain that any gardener, anywhere in the United States, will tell you that he's got adverse soil and weather conditions, too. But few places can compare to the odds that the high desert gardener has to overcome. The climate, the water supply and the soil all determine, to a great extent, the activities of the high desert gardener.

The most obvious problem in the high desert is the climate. It is dry, of course. Santa Fe, New Mexico, averages only 13.8 inches of rainfall annually. Flagstaff, Arizona, receives an average of 19.3 inches of rainfall per year.

June, when young seedlings need moist and mild weather, is usually the hottest and driest month of the year. The relative humidity often drops below 10 percent during much of June, straining vegetable crops.

Rain during the growing season usually comes in the monsoon season which, in a good year, starts in early July and ends in early September. Some years the monsoons don't start until August and last only for a few weeks.

Lack of rain is the most obvious climatic problem in the high desert, but it isn't the only one. Though average high temperatures in the summer range from the high 70s to mid-80s, the average nighttime temperatures dip into the mid to upper-50s. The cool nights are great for sleeping, but they delay the ripening of many heat-loving crops. For instance, the big, sweet and juicy tomato that is harvested in back yards thoughout America is nearly impossible to grow in the high desert — the nights are too cool.

Then there are the winds. During the spring, due to the jetstream and the wide difference between daytime and nighttime temperatures, the winds blow incessantly. They quickly rob the soil of any moisture it might have accumulated from the winter snows, and they suck the moisture out of tender seedlings. In some cases the winds are so strong they snap young seedlings in half. In most parts of the high desert, the winds subside in June and only kick up around monsoon thunderstorms.

Thunderstorms are the high desert's main source of moisture during the summer. Yet these storms can be severe and instead of dropping rain they drop hail. A hailstorm in the high desert can transform a warm July afternoon into a winter wonderland scene in a matter of minutes. Some hailstorms are so ferocious that entire gardens are wiped out, but more often than not, plants injured by hail recover and go on to produce satisfactory crops.

Along with the arid climate comes a uncertain water supply. If the sky won't give up enough water to raise vegetables, the gardener has no choice but to look to the ground water and the water table to irrigate his garden. In areas where streams flow year 'round, or where a major river runs, ditches channel the water off the stream and into the garden. In the rest of the high desert, gardeners rely on a city water system or their own wells.

In all cases, the conscientious high desert gardener must recognize water as the precious commodity that it is. This is easily done if the gardener receives a monthly water bill, but it is harder to keep in mind if one is using a well or a river. Water is a scarce and endangered resource; the high desert gardener must treat it as such.

The soil of the high desert is the result of sunshine and drought. The intense solar radiation eats up organic matter in the soil, while the lack of rain allows calcium carbonate to build up. The result is an alkaline soil with a low organic matter content. This presents a problem because most vegetables prefer a neutral-to-slightly-acid soil that is rich in organic material. Much of the high desert gardener's efforts are aimed at alleviating the alkalinity problem and increasing the soil's organic matter content.

Climate, water supply and the soil are the odds that the high desert gardener has to beat in order to be successful. Perhaps "beat" isn't the proper word; rather, the high desert gardener has to adapt to the climate, respect the water supply and improve the soil in order to have a satisfying gardening experience.

# PLANTS: SOME BASIC FACTS  II

To be a good gardener, that is, one who is equipped to handle the problems that inevitably arise, it is necessary to have a fundamental understanding of plants. The person who sticks a seedling in a hole, watches it die and then complains that he just doesn't have a green thumb is a person who doesn't understand the basic needs of plants.

There are four kinds of plants that gardeners usually encounter: the annual (most vegetables), the perennial (some are vegetables, but most are ornamentals), the shrub, and the tree. Actually all plants in the world come under one of the above categories, but some plants, due to the way they reproduce or acquire food, are grouped into special categories.

An annual is a plant that germinates from seed, grows, flowers and produces seed, all in a single growing season. Most vegetables are annuals. Some annuals are hardy and reseed themselves by dropping their seeds in the fall to sprout the following spring. Other annuals are tender and require replanting every spring.

A perennial, technically speaking, is a plant that lives for three years or more. This definition includes shrubs and trees, but when a gardener speaks of perennials, he is usually talking about herbaceous (non-woody) perennials. Some favorite perennial vegetables include asparagus, chives, fennel, and rhubarb. Perennials should also be the heart of the high desert flower garden because there are many that are drought- and heat-resistant.

A shrub is a woody plant that grows from a group of stems, not from a main trunk. Some trees often resemble shrubs and many gardeners will call what is technically a tree a shrub. Lilacs are perhaps the best-loved shrub in America, and they are well-suited to high desert conditions.

A tree is a perennial that grows from a single woody stem, or trunk. A tree can be ornamental, such as a flowering crabapple, or it can be useful, such as a cottonwood for shade or an apple tree for food.

Even the beginning gardener knows that all plants have roots. Through their roots plants absorb water and nutrients. Roots also anchor plants to the soil, and in doing so, they help to prevent soil erosion, a serious problem throughout the United States. Roots help to aerate the soil. They also prevent the soil from compacting, and when they die, roots decompose and replenish the soil with organic matter and plant nutrients.

Plants use their leaves for a number of important functions, the most crucial being food production. The process through which plants produce food is called photosynthesis. Chlorophyll, the substance that gives leaves their green tints, must be present for photosynthesis to take place. The chlorophyll enables the plant to use the energy from the sun to synthesize vital carbohydrates from air, water and other essential elements. Food gardeners grow some vegetables, such as spinach and lettuce, primarily for their leaves.

Water and the essential elements are absorbed by the roots of the plant, although some water is absorbed through the leaves. From the water the plant extracts hydrogen and oxygen.

Air is absorbed through the leaves and from the air the plant extracts carbon (from carbon dioxide). The leaves release leftover oxygen back into the atmosphere, helping to replenish the earth's oxygen supply.

The other essential elements that a plant needs to survive are obtained from the soil by the roots. The most important of these elements are nitrogen, phosphorous and potassium.

Nitrogen is the leaf and growth food, and it is often thought to be the most important of the soil-borne nutrients. Nitrogen is responsible for lush growth; without it, the other elements would be useless.

Phosphorous is the fruit and flower food. It must be present in sufficient amounts for plants to produce healthy blossoms and large, tasty crops. Phosphorous is also necessary for robust growth, healthy root systems and disease resistance.

Potassium, also called potash, is necessary for the process of photosynthesis. It also protects the plant from disease, drought and cold. In essence, potassium increases a plant's hardiness.

Other essential elements that plants draw in relatively large amounts from the soil are calcium, sulfur and magnesium. These elements are all related to a plant's ability to synthesize food and build strong cells.

A number of other essential elements are used in small quantities and are commonly referred to as trace elements. Boron, chlorine, cobalt, copper, iron, manganese, molybdenum and zinc all play small but vital roles in plant growth. The absence of one of the trace minerals can cause major problems in the garden.

The flower (the plant's blossom) is the reproductive organ of the plant. Not all flowers are gaudy; some are inconspicuous while others are simply "plain". In the vegetable garden, some plants are grown for their immature flowers, such as broccoli. Others are grown for their fruit, such as the tomato, but the blossom is a crucial forerunner; no blossom, no fruit. Some flowers are perfect — they contain the male part (the stamen) and the female part (the pistil) necessary for seed production. Other flowers are

13

termed incomplete; they have only the stamen or the pistil, not both. Either way, pollen from the stamen must reach the pistil to fertilize the flower. This process is called pollination. The wind, hummingbirds, bees, butterflies, certain flies and other insects are important plant pollinators.

Of course, plants are much more complicated than the above information suggests. Volumes have been devoted to the subject of phtotosynthesis alone. For more detailed information on plant functions, the interested gardener should consult an introductory botany text. Though an intimate knowledge of plants enhances the gardening experience, it is not a necessary ingredient in becoming an good gardener.

# STARTING THE GARDEN  III

The valley I garden in was first cultivated by Pueblo Indians, and later by Spanish settlers. A native of the valley once told me that the farmers grew chili on the east side of the river and corn on the west side because the soil on the east side was sandy while the soil to the west was clay. This strategy makes sense because the water-holding quality of the clay helped to protect the thirsty corn from drought, while the chili grew better in the well-drained sand.

The majority of us don't have the pick of an entire river valley for situating our vegetable gardens. Usually the garden has to fit somewhere in the front or back yard and finding the right site can be difficult.

There are a number of criteria that can influence the choice of a vegetable garden site, and it is rare when a site can be found that meets each criterion satisfactorily. Therefore, the most important criteria have to be met first.

Light is probably the most critical consideration when choosing a site for the garden. Soil can be improved but the sun's path across the sky can't be changed. Vegetable gardens do best on eight to 10 hours of sunlight a day so, ideally, the garden should be placed in the open, away from structures, trees, shrubs and anything else that might block the sun. However, the ideal is not always possible and compromises must be made.

If space dictates that the garden must be placed against a structure of some sort — a house or a wall — the exposure must be considered. Do not place a vegetable garden on the north side of a structure, as it will not receive enough light. The east side of a structure isn't much better because the sun only lingers there a little longer. The north and east sides of structures are shady places where shade-loving shrubs and perennials should be planted. However, if vegetable growing space is limited, the east side can be used for shade-tolerant vegetables such as spinach and lettuce.

As far as a western exposure is concerned, it is the quality of the light rather than the quantity that makes it less than desirable. Western exposures receive lots of hot, afternoon sun that can bake a garden by overheating the soil and stressing the plants.

A southern exposure is the best choice for a vegetable garden site if it has to be adjacent to a structure. There it will get good light and plenty of it. At night the garden will stay warmer as the structure releases heat that it

15

absorbed during the day. This extra warmth is an advantage in the high desert where nights are too cool to ripen some vegetables.

If a southern exposure isn't available, a southeastern exposure is the next best choice. A southwestern exposure is suitable, too, but it will have to be planned carefully so crops that prefer some shade don't receive too much of the afternoon sun.

Keep the garden site as far away from trees and shrubs as possible. Trees and shrubs that are too close to the garden will compete with the vegetables for nutrients and water, and the shade from large trees can be detrimental. Some tree roots will become very invasive, making cultivation difficult (if not impossible) and a few trees even exude a substance from their roots that inhibits other types of plant growth. If you must plant near trees and shrubs, make sure they are at least 10 feet away. Keep larger trees even farther away.

If, after considering the light and the proximity of trees and shrubs, there is only one suitable site for the garden, the decision making stops at this point. If there are a number of potential sites, start to consider the soil. Even the worst soils can be improved, but it is preferable to have a choice between a lousy soil and a slightly better one.

Take a shovel and pick ax and dig the soil to a depth of at least 16 inches at each potential garden site. Sometimes the ground will be very hard and the pick ax will be necessary to break it up. If the soil does eventually yield to the ax, there's no problem. If the shovel and ax can't get down to 16 inches, then there's a problem. Often the soil will be loose for six inches or so and then, wham — the shovel hits an unyielding layer of soil. This layer, often referred to as a hardpan, is more often than not a layer of caliche, the bane of the Southwest. Unlike a true soil hardpan, which is highly compacted soil, caliche is an almost impermeable mineral that is close to impossible to break up.

Having a layer of caliche at depths of 16 inches and less really puts a damper on the garden site. The caliche does not allow roots to penetrate it (tree roots often take 10 years to break through a caliche layer) nor does this mineral allow water to drain.

How to solve the caliche problem has puzzled many Southwestern agriculturists over the years. Some people suggest adding crushed gypsum to the soil. Big farmers can afford to bring in heavy equipment to pulverize the stuff (and that doesn't always work). Recently, an enzyme that is advertised as being able to soften caliche has appeared on the market. Caliche, however, is a calcified mineral and it seems doubtful that anything could really cure a caliche problem. But you never know until you try, and a gardener plagued by caliche is often willing to take a gamble or two.

If there is a choice, choose a site that doesn't have caliche. Frequently, one part of the yard will have caliche but another part won't have any at all. If none of the sites are caliche-free, choose the site where the caliche layer is deeper than 16 inches. If there is no such site, choose the place with the best light and prepare for a lot of work.

At this point, if there are still a couple of suitable sites, take a close look at the quality of the soil. Is it sandy or is it mostly clay? Wet the soil and roll some between your fingers. If the soil is very plastic and sticks together after it's been rolled, the soil has a high clay content. If the soil is very crumbly and falls apart (or barely stays together) after it's been rolled, it has a high sand content. Both types of soil can be improved, so the decision comes down to just how sandy or clayey the soil is. If one of the sites has very sandy soil and the other has a moderately sandy soil, choose the more moderate of the soils. It will be easier to improve. If one site is a heavy clay and the other site is very sandy, I would choose the clay site. They will both be difficult to improve but the clay holds water better and in the high desert, that's an important quality.

If there is still a choice of sites that all receive good light, have no caliche and soils of equal quality, the next thing to consider is the wind. If one of the sites is protected from prevailing winds by a wall or by trees (well away from the garden's perimeters, of course), then choose that site. Winds are extremely troublesome in the high desert, especially in the spring when seeds are trying to germinate and tender seedlings are struggling to survive.

If there isn't a site that's better protected from the wind than the other sites, consider the site's location in relation to the house. Some landscapers feel that the vegetable garden should be separated from the "living areas" of the yard. That is, the garden should be harvested but not seen. While it is true that gardens can look a bit disheveled at times, rarely is there such a thing as an unsightly garden. A productive garden becomes an integral part of summer life, and it is much more convenient for the gardener (and

17

the cook) to take a short stroll to the garden rather than a hike.

Gardens can be screened from full view by sending climbing flowers such a nasturtiums and morning glories up the fence. Or the fence can be prettied up with stained wood and decorations. As for compost piles and manure, well, compost piles rarely smell and they don't have to be near the garden. They can be placed in an obscure corner of the yard. Manure is usually spread in the late fall when the weather is cool and the windows are closed.

When the site is finally chosen, the next big decision is how the garden will be dug. This may sound odd to the novice who remembers his parents just turning over the soil and planting the seeds. Times have changed and so have gardening techniques.

In recent years, a lot of research has been done on how to improve yields with improved cultivation techniques. Much of the research has been aimed toward the needs of urban and suburban gardeners whose space is limited. The result of this research is soil preparation techniques that allow for high yields from small areas. That doesn't mean, however, that gardeners with lots of space can't take advantage of these techniques also.

One of the most popular new gardening techniques is the raised-bed garden. Actually raised beds are anything but new — the ancient Greeks used them — but modern research has improved the raised-bed method to a great extent. This is a stroke of good fortune because, in my opinion, raised-bed gardening is the best way to grow vegetables in the high desert.

Raised beds have a lot of advantages. First of all, they are dug to a depth of 24 inches which allows plant roots to travel deep into the soil after water and trace minerals. This deep-rooting makes plants resistant to drought and it also helps the plants anchor themselves more securely, which is important in the windy high desert.

The soil in a raised-bed is well aerated which promotes the growth of healthy root systems and healthy soil. Raised beds aren't walked on so the soil doesn't compact, a plus in a place where soil compaction is a fact of life.

Because fertilizers and water are applied only to the beds (not to the paths between them), there is very little waste of resources. The beds are perfectly suited to drip irrigation because once the system is in it never has to be changed. The beds don't move every year like rows in a standard garden. Only the crops grown in the beds are changed. And, contrary to popular belief, rain doesn't roll off the rounded surface of a raised bed. The soil is so loose and porous, rain is absorbed quickly and easily.

A raised-bed garden should begin on paper. Lay out the garden in beds that have a width of anywhere from two-to-four feet and length that suits the size and shape of the garden plot. Keep in mind that you will be standing, squatting or sitting in the garden paths while you work on the plants in

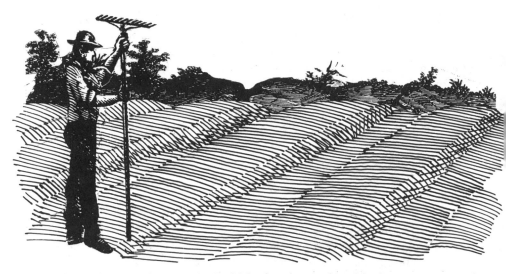

the bed, so settle on a bed width that is comfortable for your personal reach. Also remember that the beds will be difficult to jump across, so if you don't like the idea of having to walk short distances around the bed to get to the other side, you may want to make your beds short with pathways every five or 10 feet. Paths between beds should be 18 to 24 inches wide — the wider paths are more comfortable. Any main paths should be at least two feet wide to accomodate wheelbarrows. The beds can run east-west or north-south.

The best way to make raised beds is by the double-digging method, a technique introduced by the late garden researcher Alan Chadwick. Start by laying out the beds with sticks and strings. Starting at one end of a bed, dig a trench 12 inches deep and one foot wide across the width of the bed. Put the soil that is removed into a wheelbarrow. Then, with a spading fork or a pick ax (I prefer the pick ax), loosen the soil at the bottom of the trench to a depth of another 12 inches, but do not remove it. The soil does not have to be chopped up, just well loosened. Then, directly adjacent to the first trench, dig another one-foot wide by 12-inch deep trench across the width of the bed, putting the soil that is removed into the first trench. Loosen the next 12 inches of soil at the bottom of the second trench and move on to the third trench, repeating the exact same process, putting the soil that is removed into the second trench. Continue in this manner to the end of the bed. Use the soil in the wheelbarrow to fill the last trench.

Making a double-dug bed is a lot of strenuous work (and a good way to get in shape). Expect that each four-foot by 20-foot bed will take eight to 10 hours to complete. This investment of time and energy will be paid back because raised beds require much less work to maintain than a standard garden plot requires. Don't try to do the beds in one big rush. I dug the first nine four-foot by 30-foot beds of my garden over a 6-month period, starting in late fall and finishing in early spring. Those two times of the year are good times to dig beds because the soil is usually slightly damp and easy to work with and the weather is cool. Do not try to dig beds in bone-dry soil or soil that is very soggy.

Raised beds are really the way to go when growing vegetables in the high desert, but if they seem like too much trouble (which they aren't) the garden can be dug in the conventional manner. Turn the entire plot as deeply as possible. A rototiller makes this job easy, but it can be done by hand. A drip irrigation system can be used with excellent results in a standard, flat garden.

If the garden site has a shallow layer of caliche, the best thing to do is to dig the soil as deeply as possible and remove the soil from the bed. Then build beds by using frames two to three feet high. The frames can be made of railroad ties, scrap wood or stones — anything that will hold up to the weight of soil. On the bottom of the bed, spread a layer of gravel to help improve water drainage. Then fill the bed with a mixture of the soil you removed, good top soil and lots of compost and rotted manure. It is probable that you will have to purchase top soil. Before buying, ask the supplier where the soil comes from and then make sure that the area has not been treated with pesticides, herbicides or other chemicals. In some places there are suppliers of organic materials such as humus, compost and good topsoil. These products may be a bit more expensive, but they are worth the investment.

Now that a site has been found for the garden and the plot has been dug, it is time to take a closer look at the soil. Soil is the foundation of any garden. Proper maintenance is usually the difference between a so-so garden and a successful garden.

High desert soils are problematic. We've already been introduced to caliche, a soil problem that is difficult to solve. But even without the caliche, high desert soils have little to brag about. They are usually tough and poor, devoid of the qualities that are essential to growing healthy vegetables.

Good soil is a living, breathing conglomeration of ingredients. It is mainly composed of minerals but it also contains air, water, organic matter, microorganisms and other larger organisms such as earthworms, grubs

and ants. When combined in the proper proportions, these ingredients create a soil that is healthy enough to meet the demands of a vegetable garden.

Most soils in the high desert don't have the proper mix of the above ingredients. The majority of them are lacking in water, of course, and in organic matter. Most have an imbalance of mineral constituents that make them either too sandy or too clayey.

A sandy soil is dominated by relatively large, coarse particles. When it is wet and squeezed, sandy soil has a hard time holding its shape and if it manages to do that, it falls apart at the slightest touch. Because of the coarseness of a sandy soil, water drains rapidly, leaving a dry, crumbly soil behind. Sandy soils heat up rapidly and lose much of their organic matter to that heat, as well as to leaching.

A clay soil is dominated by miniscule particles that can only be seen with a powerful microscope. These particles, called colloids, adhere to each other and give clay soils their plastic qualities. When wet, a clay soil will feel slippery and will hold its shape when squeezed. When it is dry, a clay soil is extremely hard. Clay soils drain slowly and are easily waterlogged. The poor drainage causes the soil to be poorly aerated and that discourages the growth of microorganisms and the decomposition of organic matter.

Loam soils are the ideal soils. Perfect blends of sand and clay (about 50 percent sand and 10 percent clay), they also have significant quantities of silt — fine mineral particles that are smaller than sand and larger than clay. Because loams have such a good balance of coarse and fine particles, they are better aerated than clay soils and they hold water better than sandy soils. This encourages healthy populations of the microorganisms that contribute to the fertitlity of the soil. If a loam has a good percentage of organic matter — five percent is ideal — then it is a perfect soil.

Whether you have a sandy soil, a clay soil or a loam deficient in organic matter, the idea behind soil building is to create a soil that has all the properties of a perfect loam. Clay soil can be modified somewhat with the addition of sand, but it is hard to modify a sandy soil with the additon of clay, and it is not recommended. And even if you add some sand to a clay soil, that isn't enough to improve it. Other things have to be added to bring a poor soil up to standards.

When looking at a handful of soil, it is difficult to believe that there are complicated biochemical reactions taking place. It is even more surprising to learn that many of those reactions are essential to soil and plant health. Reactions between humus (decomposed organic matter), minerals and chemical elements in the soil determine whether nutrients present there will be in forms readily available to plants.

Clay colloids and particles of humus are the main areas of biochemical activity in the soil. Their surface charges attract nutrient ions and hold them, protecting the soil against leaching. Due to their surface charges, clay colloids and humus particles also help to maintain the granular structure of a good soil.

Organic matter provides the material for humus and it is the source of major nutrients, including nitrogen, phosphorous and sulfur. Organic matter also improves the water-holding ability of a soil, and it provides food for soil microorganisms as they break it down into humus.

Obviously, organic matter is an essential ingredient for a healthy soil. Since most high desert soils lack in organic matter, the first order of business after the garden has been dug is to add organic matter. This is a simple process that is *absolutely essential* to gardening in the high desert. As you will learn, the maintenance of a good level of organic matter in the soil solves a lot of common high desert gardening problems.

The most common sources of organic matter are farm animal manures. Horse, steer, goat, sheep and chicken manures are all suitable for the garden. Horse, goat, sheep and rabbit manures are the best choices because they are easy to handle and break down quickly. Steer manure is hard to handle and can take a long time to break down into a form suitable

for direct application to the garden. Chicken manure is extremely potent and should be mixed with coop bedding (usually straw) and aged before it is applied to the garden. Steer and chicken manures are better saved for the compost heap.

Fresh manures are best added to the garden in the fall. They should never be added to the soil less than six weeks before planting time. That is why, for the best results, the optimal time for starting a garden is in the fall. At that time large amounts of manure can be worked into the soil and allowed to mellow over the winter.

Aged manure can be added to the garden in the spring. In most cases, aged manure has been allowed to sit for two to three months. Steer manure and chicken manure should sit for at least six months. When using aged manure it is best to add it to the soil two or three weeks before planting. After the manure has been added, keep the soil moist to encourage decomposition. If you are unsure as to whether the manure has aged enough, use the sniff test. If it smells very strongly of manure let it age some more. If there is only a hint of manure in its smell, it's ready to use.

Be liberal when adding manure, especially when starting the garden. A one-inch layer spread on the garden is good, but a three-inch layer is better. In succeeding years, resupply the soil with a one-inch layer every fall after harvest.

After the manure has been spread, turn it into the soil, but not too deeply. Keep it in the top six to 12 inches, where plants can take advantage of it. As the manure decomposes, it will eventually find its way deeper into the soil where it will help to improve structure and water retention.

In the high desert, when manure is added to the garden in the fall, it is advantageous to turn most of it in while saving a little to spread as a thin layer on the soil surface. This layer will act as a mulch and help to retain any moisture the soil picks up during the winter. A soil that has been protected by a thin layer of manure will be damp and easy to work with in the spring.

Getting manure usually isn't a problem. People who keep horses will often let you dig out the stables once a month. A friend who raises chickens would probably be more than happy to let you clean out the coop. Cleaning stables may not sound like the most pleasant of chores, but it can be fun if done with friends or family. Dress in old clothes and enjoy the chance to be outdoors and communing with the animals. And, if you don't want to haul manure, there are plenty of people who will haul it for you...for a fee.

A few notes of caution. Don't take manure mixed with sawdust. As the sawdust decomposes, it binds up available nitrogen, making it unavailable to plants. Also, don't take manure from feed lots. Animals in feed lots are fed a high proportion of rich grains that make their manure very salty. Salt can build up in soils and destroy the chemical balance necessary for healthy soils and healthy plants. So, it is a good idea to ask about the diet of the animals before hauling the manure.

## COMPOST

A gardener's life would be simple if adding manure to the soil was all that was necessary to improve it. Although manure goes a long way toward improving the soil, it isn't enough to add manure alone. Compost is a remarkable soil improver, and it is especially important for successful high desert gardening.

Humus is a major determinant of nutrient availability and soil structure. Compost is purposely-created humus. Instead of leaving it up to nature to break down whatever organic material might be around, gardeners concentrate these materials in the compost heap. The result is a humus that has major nutrients, trace elements and soil improvers, all readily available to plants.

There are three basic components in a compost heap. A nitrogen source is needed to provide the fuel that microorganisms need to change organic-matter into simpler forms. Two of the best and readily accessible sources of nitrogen for the compost pile are fresh manure and fresh grass clippings.

Other types of organic matter must be included in the compost heap to provide carbon, trace minerals and food for the microorganisms. Plant residues (roots, leaves and stems), most kitchen scraps, straw and other dry vegetation make up the carbon-rich ingredients of the compost. Avoid bark and sawdust because they inhibit decomposition.

The third ingredient in compost is soil. Soil provides the microorganisms necessary for decomposition, plus it helps to keep odor down.

Situate the compost away from living areas. A bin can be constructed to contain the pile. A set of two bins is a better arrangement so more than one pile can be going at the same time. Build the bins out of chicken wire, scrap wood, cinder blocks or anything else that's sturdy. The bins don't have to be large — four-foot-by-four-foot is a good, manageable dimension. The bins don't need lids and they can have three or four sides. A four-sided compost bin has the advantage of closing out curious dogs, cats and children, but one of the sides should be removable so the bin is easy to use.

To start the compost, chop up the soil that the heap will rest on. This exposes soil microorganisms. Wet down the soil and spread a three-inch layer of carbon-rich ingredients and sprinkle on a few handfuls of bone meal. Wet this layer down and then spread a three-inch layer of nitrogen-rich ingredients sprinkled with a few handfuls of blood meal. (Both bone meal and blood meal are by-products of the meatpacking industry.) Wet the nitrogen layer and then spread a one-inch layer of soil on top of it. Repeat this process until ingredients run out or until the pile reaches a height of four feet.

There are many variations on this simple compost recipe. Some gardeners make the layers thinner, while others make the nitrogen layer thicker than the other layers. Some gardeners do not supplement their compost heaps with bone meal or blood meal.

Within a few days after the compost heap is constructed, it will begin to heat up. The heat is energy that is released by the microorganisms during decomposition. Optimally, the heat at the center should reach 160 degrees F. to kill insect eggs, larvae and many weed seeds. This doesn't always happen and there's no need to worry about it. A cooler pile will take a longer time to finish but it will be just as good.

The hardest thing about successful compost-making in the high desert is keeping the pile damp. If the compost isn't wet enough, it won't cook at all. When building the compost heap, make sure each layer is liberally wetted down. After the pile has been made, it will dry out rapidly in the desert air. The best way to prevent its drying is to lay a hose on top of the pile and let it drip very slowly for a few hours a week. Or a line can be run from an existing drip irrigation system to the pile. Either way, be careful not to overwater the compost or the microorganisms will suffocate.

Because the microorganisms need oxygen to do their work efficiently, it is necessary to turn the compost. Every two to three weeks, take a pitchfork and turn the pile so that the ingredients on the top end up in the center and the ingredients for the center wind up on the outside of the pile. The pile will take a couple of days to get hot again.

Compost can take anywhere from eight to 16 weeks to finish, depending on the ingredients and the time of year. A heap that is made all at once and gets very hot is usually done in eight to 10 weeks and sometimes even sooner. Sometimes a pile is constructed little by little when sufficient amounts of kitchen wastes are available. These piles cook slowly, need to be turned more frequently and benefit from extra helpings of nitrogen. This "add-on" type of compost can take as long as 12 to 16 weeks to finish.

Finished compost is dark and crumbly, and it smells clean and earthy, like a good forest soil. And, in essence, composting is nothing more than copying nature's own way of recycling the things that fall to the forest floor.

A few words about compost ingredients. Save all kitchen scraps except for meats and very greasy foods. If there are a lot of curious dogs in the neighborhood, you might want to avoid adding bones, even though they are excellent for the compost. Be sure to save coffee grounds and tea leaves; they are both excellent soil acidifiers. Tea bags decompose if the string, tag and staples are removed. Also, be sure to include citrus peels and egg shells.

Kitchen scraps can be saved in a garbage can outside. When the can is full, the contents can be used to build a heap. That method gets rather smelly, especially in the summer, and the ingredients freeze solid in the winter. An alternative is to keep a two-quart plastic container in the kitchen to catch all wastes and then empty it onto the compost heap whenever it gets full. This is the basis of the add-on pile. When the wastes build into a two-inch layer, put a nitrogen rich layer on top of them, add a layer of soil and start all over.

When using grass clippings — a rare commodity in many parts of the high desert — be very sure that the lawn was not treated with pesticides, herbicides or chemical fertilizers. These potent chemicals can ruin the compost and the garden. This same precaution also holds true for soil. The soil used in a compost heap doesn't have to be good garden soil, but be careful not to use contaminated soil.

Compost can be added to the soil at any time. In the fall and spring, one-inch layers of finished compost can be spread on the garden and turned into the top six inches of soil. If plants seem to need a boost during the growing season, compost can be added then. There's no limit on the amount of compost that can be added to the garden — you can't add too much of nature's perfect fertilizer. The thing to remember is that compost is indispensible to the high desert gardener, so USE IT!

## GREEN MANURES

Another excellent way to add organic matter to the soil is to grow green manures. How, you may wonder, does a gardener grow manure if he doesn't own animals? Well, green manures are plant residues, not animal wastes, so they are very simple to grow. The only thing needed is time.

Green manures are grains and legumes that are grown only to be turned back into the soil. When they are tilled under, green manures add organic matter to the soil and as they decompose, they increase the soil's supply of humus. Green manures are an excellent way to bring poor soil up to vegetable garden standards. The only problem is that the soil is out of production while green manures are growing.

Many grains and legumes make good green manures. Sweet white clover and alfalfa are good leguminous green manures for high desert gardens. Legumes have a symbiotic relationship with a certain bacteria in the soil, and because of that relationship, legume roots take nitrogen from the air and "fix" it in the soil. Therefore, legumes actually add nitrogen to the soil rather than deplete the existing supply.

Buckwheat, oats and rye are good non-leguminous green manures. Buckwheat, if allowed to flower, attracts bees and is said to break up a hardpan (not caliche). All non-leguminous crops produce more top growth than legumes and add more organic matter to the soil when tilled under.

To plant green manures, prepare a smooth seed bed and set a number of buckets of sifted soil aside. It is a good idea to add manure to the soil before planting, but green manures are planted to improve the soil and will tolerate poor soils. Broadcast the seeds as evenly as possible and cover them with a thin layer of soil (no more than one-inch thick). Water the seed bed with a gentle spray and make sure the bed stays damp until the seeds have germinated. Then make sure the crop has sufficient water during the growing season.

Alfalfa, sweet clover, oats and rye can be planted anytime from spring through fall. Rye is especially tough and will stay green most of the winter.

In late winter it will start to green up again. Buckwheat, on the other hand, is a warm weather green manure and should be planted in June.

The green manure can be tilled under any time after it is a few inches high. Since the crop is being grown for organic matter, it is advantageous to let it get pretty tall. Most gardeners till under green manures just before they flower; however it is okay to let them flower and then till them. Do not let the crop go to seed. A rototiller is the easiest and most efficient way to turn under a green manure. Muscle power also works, but it's much slower and doesn't chop the plants as well as a tiller does.

Because green manures are so high in nitrogen, they decompose very rapidly once they've been turned into the soil. Usually it only takes a month for the plants to decompose. Vegetables can be planted after the green manure has decomposed. Rye grows so rapidly in the early spring, it can be turned under and decomposed long before the major spring planting.

## EARTHWORMS

The last type of soil improver I want to discuss is the lowly earthworm. This little critter is the gardener's garbage disposal because it travels through the soil, eating non-living organic matter. The earthworm is one of nature's best composters. Its manure, called castings, is rich in nitrogen, calcium, potassium, phosphorous and trace minerals. It has been estimated that an earthworm produces its own weight in castings every 24 hours and in good soil, earthworms produce 50 tons of fertilizer per acre. Through their travels, earthworms aerate the soil, preventing its compaction and they can even break up a soil hardpan.

High desert soils are woefully lacking in earthworms. This is especially true of over-grazed soils and soils where the topsoil has been scraped away. Luckily, earthworms are easy to import. Once the garden is started and the soil is damp, earthworms will sometimes appear by themselves. If that doesn't happen, go to the side of a stream or river and dig around in the soil. You are bound to run into a few earthworms, often called night crawlers. Collect a can of worms, take them home and introduce them to the garden by burying them in some damp soil. If you can't find earthworms in the wild, check bulletin boards in feed stores or look in the classified ads for an earthworm farmer. He or she will be happy to sell you earthworms by the pint or pound.

# SOIL pH   V

Understanding soil pH is a crucial part of gardening, especially in the high desert. Most people have heard the term "pH" before, but are baffled by its scientific sound. Actually, pH is an easy idea to grasp.

pH is simply the scale that is used to measure the degree of acidity or alkalinity of a substance. Everything has a pH. Thus, soil pH is the degree of acidity or alkalinity of the soil. The funny "pH" symbol stands for potential hydrogen, a measure of hydrogen ionization, something that isn't necessary to understand when working in a backyard garden.

pH runs on a scale from 0 to 14. "0" is the most acidic, "14" is the most alkaline (or basic) and "7" is neutral. Most vegetables prefer a soil that has a pH between 6.5 and 7.0 At that pH, all essential plant nutrients are in forms that are available to plants. At higher or lower pHs, some nutrients are "bound up" in forms that are unavailable to plants.

The problem in the high desert is that soil pH normally runs at 8.0 and often higher. This is due, for the most part, to the lack of leaching from rain (soils in the East are leached too much and tend to be too acidic). At a pH of 8.0 some of the phosphorous, iron, zinc and manganese becomes locked into forms that a plant cannot use. The degree to which each of these nutrients are unavailable to plants depends on the nutrient and the exact pH, but iron is usually the first crucial nutrient to become completely locked up.

Iron deficiency, call chlorosis, is a common problem in high desert gardens, orchards and in non-native ornamental trees and shrubs. Chlorosis is easily identified. Leaves become very yellow while the veins in the leaves remain dark green. In evergreens, needles take on this characteristic lemon-yellow. Memorize these symptoms so that you can recognize chlorosis immediately.

To find the pH of the soil, purchase a pH test kit. There are kits in all price ranges, but if you plan to get fairly serious about gardening, purchase a complete soil test kit. There are also automatic pH gauges that measure the pH on a little scale when a special probe is placed in the soil. These gadgets are said to be quite accurate and are very easy to use.

If the soil pH is too high — above 7.0 — and there's a good chance it will be, steps will have to be taken to solve this problem.

Many high desert gardeners have turned to iron sulfate, iron chelates or sulfur (and the chemical fertilizer ammonium sulfate) to solve the pH problem, mistakenly thinking that these chemical additives are cures. The chemicals do work by immediately alleviating the problem of iron deficiency and temporarily lowering the pH but they are expensive and they will have to be applied year after year, if not more often. These chemical soil modifiers are quick fixes and will do in an emergency, but the smart high desert gardener should not depend on them to solve the pH problem.

If you've already added manure and/or green manure to the soil, you've taken a major step toward solving the pH dilemma. The chemical reactions during the decomposition of organic matter are acidic. Compost is also acidic, especially if a lot of coffee grounds and tea leaves have been included. By keeping the soil well-stocked with organic matter and compost, the pH will go down and stay down.

If organic matter and compost have been added and given at least a few weeks to work and the pH remains too high, there are other things that can be done. This particular situation is typical of first-year gardens. Often it takes a full year of use to really incorporate compost and organic matter into the soil's life cycle.

Certain organic soil modifiers are acidifying. One of these is cottonseed meal. This nitrogen-rich product can be added to the soil at a rate of no more than five pounds per hundred square feet. You will find that cottonseed meal is expensive. A relatively new soil acidifier, called "Clodbuster," is 15 percent humic acid and has a pH of 5.5. Apply it at a rate of no more than one pound per one hundred square feet. If you are lucky enough to have access to decomposed pine needles or oak leaves, these will also lower the pH.

If, during the course of the growing season, the garden experiences a rise in the pH, then the quick-fix approach will be necessary. This often occurs in first-year gardens; beans — especially pole beans — are usually the first plants (and sometimes the only ones) to indicate a pH problem by becoming chlorotic. I prefer to use iron chelates but iron sulfate will also work. Follow application instructions on the package.

If you are diligent about adding organic matter and compost to the soil, the use of the above-mentioned organic and chemical acidifiers will probably be unnecessary after the garden's first season. This is why organic gardening is so well suited to the high desert. The maintenance of high levels of organic matter in the soil usually solves the soil problems found in the high desert.

# FERTILIZERS VI

A fertilizer is any substance that increases the nutrient level of a soil. Most people associate fertilizer with heavy bags of chemicals that have a set of three numbers on the front. Be it 10-6-4 or 10-10-10, the set of numbers is the analysis of the fertilizer in terms of its nitrogen (N), phosphorous (P), and potassium (K) content. These three numbers are the gardener's trusty "NPK" rating, and they come on synthetic and natural fertilizers.

The use of synthetic fertilizers has many drawbacks. The production of these substances is based on petroleum, a non-renewable resource, so they can get pretty expensive. Synthetic fertilizers provide a lot of immediately available nutrients all at once, much more than the plants can actually use. Much of the unused fertilizer leaches away because the soil humus does not hold it well. Because it leaches so easily, synthetic fertilizer has to be applied to the garden a number of times during the growing season, and that can be expensive.

A more costly side effect of synthetic fertilizer is its effect on the soil. Because it is so potent, a synthetic fertilizer can use up the energy of vital soil microorganisms by giving them too much to eat too fast. Some synthetic fertilizers can be toxic to certain soil microorganisms. Without the microorganisms, the organic matter in the soil cannot be decomposed. Also the application of large amounts of immediately available nutrients tends to weaken plants by stimulating excess growth. All in all, synthetic fertilizers destroy the vitality of the soil and make plants more susceptible to disease and pests.

Since the idea in high desert gardening is to build up the soil and maintain its health, synthetic fertilizers have no place in the high desert garden.

Compost and organic matter contain many nutrients. but it is important that these soil improvers are supplemented with more concentrated sources of the three major nutrients, especially during the first few seasons of a new garden. After a few years of good soil maintenance, the garden's need for additional fertilizers will drop substantially. This is especially true when the compost used in the garden is made from the garden's wastes — old, spent plants and the like. By recycling the garden's product, you replace a lot of the nutrients that the plants removed earlier in the season. There are plenty of natural sources of nitrogen, phosphorous and potassium. Some are expensive but they are slow-releasing and provide long-term supplies that don't leach from the soil. Organic fertilizers are applied in smaller amounts than synthetic fertilizers and they last longer. So in the long run, organic fertilizers cost less than synthetic fertilizers.

The most efficient way to learn what nutrients the soil needs is to perform a soil test with a good test kit. This may save you some money by showing that some nutrients are in good supply. However, many people have gardened organically for years without ever performing a test and have gotten excellent results. In the beginning, it is wise to assume that your high desert soil has poor supply of nitrogen and phosphorous, two of the major nutrients, and the maximum amounts of each of these nutrients should be applied to the soil. In the third season, these amounts can be decreased until by the fifth or sixth gardening season, very little extra fertilizer is being added. If you do decide to test, check the soil before the planting season in the spring, or after the major fall harvest.

The most readily available organic source of nitrogen is blood meal. Feed stores usually stock it in large bags, compared to the small one-pound bags found at nurseries. Buying in large quantities is cheaper. Blood meal is rich in nitrogen and is fairly quick acting, and it provides nitrogen for three to four months (almost an entire growing season). The maximum application is five pounds per 100 square feet. Do not apply more than three pounds per 100 square feet within two weeks of planting or plants may burn.

Another common organic source of nitrogen is cottonseed meal. This has the added advantage of acidifying the soil. Cottonseed meal's effectiveness lasts from four to six months and up to 10 pounds per 100 square feet can be applied.

Other organic sources of nitrogen are hoof and horn meal, and fish meal. Hoof and horn meal, a by-product of the meat-packing industry, is sometimes found in feed stores. It is very slow-releasing and does not take effect for at least a month after it is applied. However, it lasts for one year. The maximum rate of application is four pounds per 100 square feet.

Fish meal is a rather inappropriate fertilizer for the high desert since there are no canneries or the like in the desert. Fish meal purchased in the high desert may be expensive, if it is available at all. Apply it at a rate of no more than five pounds per 100 square feet.

Steamed bone meal is the most common source of phosphorous and the easiest to come by. It is released slowly and remains effective for one year. Apply bone meal at a rate of no more than five pounds per 100 square feet. Bone meal can be purchased at feed stores and is also a good source of calcium. Make sure that bone meal purchased at nurseries is not adulterated with ammonium phosphate, a synthetic source of phosphorous.

A source of phosphorous that has become difficult to find in the high desert is rock phosphate (or phosphate rock). Because it is very slow-releasing, rock phosphate must be added to the soil three or four months before planting time — some time in late fall or early winter. Rock phosphate needs to react with acids released by humus in order to release its phosphorous so it is most effective in soils that have been generously enriched with organic matter and compost. Applied at a rate of up to 10 pounds per 100 square feet, rock phosphate will last for three to five years. Unfortunately, rock phosphate is very heavy. This makes it expensive to ship and raises its cost to consumers in areas where it is not mined. Many nurseries and farm suppliers have stopped carrying this excellent product. It is my favorite source of phosphorous.

Potassium (also called potash) is not a big problem for high desert soil; arid regions in the United States are known for their good supply of soil potash. Normally, the potash that is added through organic matter and compost is all that is needed to supplement a high desert garden. Peels from vegetables and fruits, especially citrus peels, are high in potassium and should be included in the compost heap.

If for some reason potash levels are low, the best way to supplement it is with greensand or granite dust. Greensand has a higher potash content than granite dust as well as higher content of trace minerals. Greensand also has an excellent water-holding ability, an important plus in the high desert. Both granite dust and greensand can be applied at a rate of up to 10 pounds per 100 square feet, although this maximum rate is probably much too much for the high desert. Because they are minerals, apply these fertilizers three to four months before planting time. Both greensand and granite dust last for 10 years.

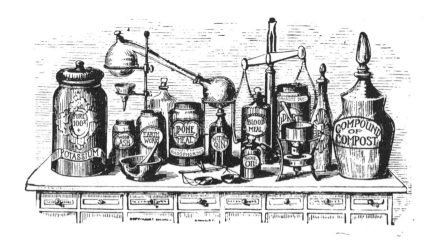

People who are used to gardening in the East will often recommend wood ashes for a potash supplement. This is bad advice. For one thing, wood ashes are quickly leached from the soil. The other problem is that wood ashes are very alkaline, a quality not welcome in high desert soils. If the garden should experience an acute potash shortage during the growing season, wood ashes can be used at a rate of one pound per 100 square feet as a stop-gap measure. After applying them, make sure to soak the garden well so that the ashes will leach as quickly as possible and not do too much damage to the pH.

Since organic supplements are safe materials, they can be applied by hand. Weigh out the quantity you want to apply and cast it gently across the soil surface. Apply the fertilizers as evenly as possible and, for obvious reason, avoid spreading them on windy days. After the fertilizer has been applied, use a spading fork or shovel to turn them into the top three inches of the soil.

Be forewarned that bone meal attracts dogs and should be stored in a shed or in a dog-proof container. Blood meal, on the other hand, usually repels all animals and is a good defense against rabbits, gophers and deer if it is spread around the perimeter of the garden.

During the growing season, you may want to boost your plants' growth with an extra addition of fertilizer. This type of supplementary fertilization is called side-dressing. To side-dress a plant or a row of plants, carefully dig a shallow trench (no deeper than two inches) about two inches from small plants like spinach and lettuce, or four inches from large plants like tomatoes. Fill the trench with fertilizer, cover it with soil and water to start the nutrients on their way. Leafy crops, such as spinach and lettuce, benefit from a side-dressing of blood meal to boost leaf production. Tomatoes often appreciate a side-dressing of compost laced with bone meal in the middle of the season, just as it begins to set fruit. The side-dressing technique can be used to apply wood ashes in the case of a potash shortage in a few plants.

Manure tea is an excellent nitrogen-rich side-dressing. To make manure tea, place a few shovelfuls of fresh manure in a medium or large heavy-duty garbage can. Fill the can with water, cover and let steep for 24 hours. Apply the tea with coffee cans (or something similar) spreading it evenly along the rows, or pouring a half canful by each plant. Manure tea is not a pleasant substance but it will win your heart when you see the results.

The object of water use in the high desert is to conserve it whenever possible. There are numerous water conservation techniques that can be employed when watering the garden and orchard. Many wise, high desert dwellers are building gray-water systems into their homes so that the waste from the sink, the bathtub and the washing machine is diverted into gardens and orchards, rather than going to the septic system. Lawns should be outlawed in the high desert unless they are sown with native grasses that do not require constant watering. A bluegrass lawn demands four feet of water annually in the high desert climate. A resident of the high desert must learn to live with the limitations of the climate. Working with nature is much more rewarding than trying to outfox her.

Sprinklers are the most popular way to water the garden. But sprinklers are an inefficient and wasteful irrigation method. The worst thing about sprinklers is that much of the water delivered is lost to evaporation in the desert's dry air and never reaches the ground. Another problem with sprinklers is that areas not supporting plants get watered and what water that does get to the garden itself is not applied directly to the root zone. Water lands on leaves and some is again lost to evaporation. On top of all those drawbacks, sprinklers lightly pound the soil with water and cause it to compact.

Furrow irrigation is still popular among farmers in many parts of the high desert. This "old fashioned" type of irrigation is most commonly used when water is taken from rivers or irrigation ditches, however it is perfectly feasible to use standard garden hoses. The furrows should run between double rows of plants. Each furrow should be about eight inches deep and 12-to-24 inches wide. The more shallow the furrow, the better the water soaks into the soil. Water can be allowed to run slowly into the furrows, or the furrows can be dammed and filled with water.

Furrow irrigation isn't as wasteful as sprinklers but it is still an inefficient watering method. It requires time to manage it and the water is not applied directly to the root zones, so some water is wasted. Furrow watering works best in conventional gardens and is not well-suited to raised-bed gardens.

The best way to irrigate in the high desert is to use one of the many types of drip irrigation systems. Drip irrigation was first developed in Israel over 40 years ago when an engineer noticed that a fruit tree growing by a leaky

faucet was growing better than any of the other trees in the orchard. In the past few years, drip irrigation has been catching on among gardeners (and commercial farmers) across the country, especially in the arid regions. Higher yields from less water are the results that have been reported over and over again.

Drip irrigation provides measured amounts of water directly to the soil at a very slow rate. It does not compact the soil, nor does it flood it. Rather, because the water is applied so slowly and steadily, the soil's air supply is not temporarily upset, and a good balance of oxygen and water results.

Hose is laid through the garden and special emitters are attached to the hose, usually every 12 inches. Each emitter applies a certain amount of water per hour. Some drip one gallon per hour, while some deliver only a half gallon per hour. Other types of emitters apply as much as two gallons per hour. Because the water is gradually dripped onto the soil, it is easily absorbed and it penetrates deeply and rapidly. After I switched from a sprinkler to drip system, watering time for the garden was cut in half, so less water was used and yields were substantially higher.

Drip irrigation is perfectly suited to raised beds. It is easy to fit a system to the beds and there is no need to change the set-up from year to year because the basic garden layout stays the same. The drip system is easily expanded to meet the increased need.

A drawback to drip irrigation is that it requires an initial monetary investment. The cost of installing a drip system into a large garden runs from $150 to $200, depending on the type of system that's purchased. If you're paying water bills, the system will probably pay for itself by the end of the second season in terms of the amount of money it saves on the monthly water bill. For a gardener with his own well, the shorter watering time saves wear on the pump and, of course, it conserves water. And not to be ignored are the earlier harvests and heavier yields that usually result from drip watering.

Another drawback, albeit a minor one, is that drip irrigation doesn't promote a humid microclimate in the garden. The moisture that lands on the leaves when a sprinkler system is used is not provided by a drip system. This moisture is valuable in two ways: it attracts beneficial insects and it promotes healthy plant growth. Foggers can be attached to some types of drip systems. These devices send up a fine mist that wets the undersides of the leaves and raises the garden's humidity. Some systems don't have fogger attachments so moisture should be provided by spraying the garden with a fine mist when the sun is low in the sky. I prefer the morning. In raised-bed gardens, plants are grown close together and this substantially raises the humidity in the garden. I have found that beneficial insects show up even when I don't mist the garden regularly and by mid-season the proximity of the plants helps to keep air moisture at a good level.

Another slight drawback to the drip system is that it doesn't wet the entire surface of the soil (this is a problem with furrow irrigation, too). At planting time a hose with a spray nozzle must be used to keep the soil surface damp while seeds are germinating. Continue to use the drip system while seeds are germinating so that the young roots will be encouraged to grow deeply.

Before purchasing a drip system, shop around. Find out about the many different kinds of systems, what they can do and what they can't do, and their relative costs. Drip systems shouldn't be limited to the vegetable garden. They are perfect for orchards, ornamental trees and shrubs, flower gardens and greenhouses.

In general, most gardeners believe that the best time to water is in the evening. Personally, I've never decided whether there is an advantage to that practice or not. In the high desert there are a few negative aspects to evening watering. It cools the plants, especially if watering by a sprinkler in the latter part of the evening. With the naturally cool nights of the high desert, it isn't particularly advantageous to cool the plants even more. Also, the sun and heat can be intense in the high desert afternoons so it seems wiser to have supplied the water in the early morning to ensure against drying out later in the day.

On the other hand, when the rains come in July and August, the garden really takes off. This is noteworthy because the rain usually falls in the late afternoon and evening. So, some gardeners might feel it is wise to follow nature's lead and water late in the day. In the case of drip irrigation, the time of day is not as important because unless the system has foggers the plants don't get wet and aren't cooled by moisture on the leaves.

All in all, it doesn't seem to make much difference in the quality of the plants whether they are watered in the morning or evening. I suggest watering when it is most convenient, in the early morning or late afternoon, when the sun is low. Watering at midday is out, unless there is an emergency.

How often the garden should be watered and how much water should be supplied are important considerations. The main idea behind watering is to maintain a steady supply of water. Letting the soil get too dry before watering stresses the plants and overwatering the soil depletes the oxygen supply and slows growth.

As a general rule, the soil should be kept near its full water-holding capacity. At full capacity, the soil is holding as much water as it can without being waterlogged. When squeezed, a soil at full capacity won't release moisture but your hand will feel damp. A waterlogged soil will give off water. Usually I keep the soil near full capacity, somewhere between 75 and 90 percent, but plants will handle soils that are only at 50 percent of their water-holding capacity. The best rule to follow is do not allow the soil to dry out so that the plants are stressed.

Watching the plants is another way to judge soil moisture, but it can have some drastic results. Many plants, most notably the squash family (cucurbitaceae), will wilt during the heat of the day to conserve moisture, even when the soil has plenty of water. By evening, they pop back up. If other plants wilt and do not revive by evening, or if they wilt early in the day, then water is lacking and should be added immediately. If plants are wilting and the soil has had plenty of water, then the garden has been over-watered and oxygen has been crowded out of the soil. Sometimes one plant will suddenly wilt while the others remain erect. This is probably the result of a disease appropriately called wilt.

Learning to water and how much water to apply is a trial-and- error process. It is an easy lesson to learn and the garden probably won't suffer at all while you're learning.

# MULCH VIII

In the fields and forests, leaves, pine needles and grasses die and fall to the ground, creating a layer of mulch. This natural mulch protects the soil and its organisms from the rays of the sun, keeping the soil cool and moist. Eventually the mulch breaks down and becomes a part of the soil in the form of humus.

The use of mulch in the garden is in direct imitation of nature. Mulch protects the soil from the strong rays of the high desert sun, keeping it cool and helping to retain moisture. In this way, mulch helps to conserve water and create a microclimate around the plants, keeping humidity high and temperatures moderate. By blocking light, mulch reduces the number of weeds that appear and makes pulling them easier. Eventually the mulch breaks down and contributes organic matter to the soil. Because of these qualities, mulch is an indispensible gardening tool in the high desert.

Applying mulch is a simple process. The material is laid down loosely on top of the soil and around the plants. In time, the mulch will compact and more will have to be added.

In the spring, when the winds are high, it is very difficult to keep mulch from blowing away. This is frustrating because spring is when mulch is needed to protect against moisture loss. Sometimes mulch can be kept in place by lightly sprinkling it with soil, rotted manure or compost. More often than not, I give up trying to use mulch until the spring winds have gone or the plants have grown tall enough to hold the mulch in place.

Many materials make good mulches. The following is a list of the ones most commonly used.

**Compost:** Compost is an excellent mulch. It does all of the things a mulch is supposed to do, plus it adds readily available nutrients to the soil. As a mulch, compost should be spread about one-inch thick. That means that a lot of compost is needed to mulch a medium-sized garden. If there is a limited supply of compost, and there usually is, it is best to reserve it for adding directly to the soil in the spring or fall. Compost is a good mulch for seed beds if it is sifted and spread in a very thin layer.

**Hay:** Hay is also an excellent mulching material. Hay has a good ratio of carbon to nitrogen and it breaks down easily. Spoiled hay is the best type to use because the decomposition process has already begun. Spoiled hay is hard to come by in the dry high desert, but when it can be found, its owners will usually let it be hauled away for free. Or you can make spoiled

hay by purchasing fresh hay and wetting it down to start the decomposition process. For best results, apply the hay four inches thick. Spoiled hay is also a good ingredient for the compost heap.

**Leaves:** Dead leaves are often used as a mulch and they do a commendable job, but they have a high cellulose content which makes them slow to break down. There is also the risk that during the breakdown process the leaves will tie up the nitrogen supply. It is best to let the leaves rot for the few months before using them as mulch. Rake them in the fall, form a pile and wet it down. Turn the pile a few times during the winter, making sure it stays damp and by spring the leaves will be highly suitable for mulch. When using leaves for mulch or the compost heap, be sure to use only leaves from your immediate neighborhood. "Importing" leaves from across town, or from city to country, can import pests that weren't previously found in your area. For best results, apply leaves three inches thick.

**Paper:** Newspaper and paper bags can be used as mulch. However, they are hard to keep in place and can give the garden an unsightly appearance. A layer four sheets thick is recommended; however, shredded newspaper has been found to be more effective than sheets. Never use colored newspaper because it may contain high levels of lead.

**Plastic:** In the past 10 years or so, plastic has become a somewhat popular mulch. In my opinion, plastic is the worst choice for mulch because it is the antithesis of mulch. Gardening is a cycle that turns death and decay into life that eventually dies and decays, returning to the soil to help support new life. Mulch is a part of that cycle. However, plastic is a petroleum product. It has never lived (in modern times), nor does it die and decay. It adds nothing to the soil. It doesn't allow soil to breathe, it

40

can overheat the soil in the high desert and it repels water. And, what's more, plastic is expensive!

**Straw:** Straw is probably the most commonly used mulch. It does the job well and keeps the garden looking prim and proper. There can be a slight problem with nitrogen tie-up because some straw has a high ratio of carbon to nitrogen, but this is a rare occurence. A little manure can be added to the straw when it is put down to help prevent the problem. Oat straw is favored because it has a lower cellulose content, but other kinds of straw are acceptable. Straw's light color reflects light and speeds up the ripening of peppers, eggplants and tomatoes. Start with a layer four inches thick and add more as it compacts during the couse of the growing season.

In raised beds, crops are planted very close together and sometimes create a living mulch. As they grow and their leaves overlap, they shade the soil beneath them, keeping it cool and cutting down on evaporation. So, in certain places mulch may not be needed on raised beds, although its addition certainly couldn't hurt.

In the spring, it is important that the soil is allowed to warm up. Pull away existing mulch to expose the soil to the sun's warming rays. The desert sun is so strong that warming is usually accomplished in a week; two at most. This soil warming is especially crucial for areas of the garden where warm-weather crops are going to grow. Here is one time when plastic may be of some help. If the soil is not warming quickly, say during an unusually cool spring, lay black plastic on the soil for a week before planting time. This will warm the soil very effectively. Remove the plastic when the crops are planted. It is worthwhile to allow the soil to continue to warm up after planting by leaving it uncovered for a few weeks. Usually, by the middle of June, the weather is hot enough to mulch warm-weather crops with a cooling mulch.

Mulch also comes in handy in mid-to-late summer when fall crops are being planted. Spinach, lettuce, peas and other cool-weather crops prefer a cool soil for germination and sometimes they won't germinate at all in the warm soils of late summer. A light mulch will keep the soil cool and damp. The seedling will poke right through the mulch. Straw or hay is the best material for the job.

# PLANNING THE GARDEN IX

Most first-time gardeners don't plan their gardens. Many experienced gardeners plant their gardens haphazardly, year after year. Yet one of the most worthwhile and enjoyable things a gardener can do is to take the time to carefully map out the garden.

A thoughtfully planned garden is a better garden. With plan in hand, the gardener will know such things as how much seed to purchase, how many seedlings will be needed and where everything gets planted. A plan helps to jar the memory, and long after the garden has died, it will help to identify those varieties that did well, and those that performed poorly. And if, for instance, there wasn't enough corn, the plan will help the gardener calculate how much more she'll have to plant next season. A plan provides a lasting record of the garden, and should be kept in a safe place where it can be referred to during the season, and when planning subsequent seasons.

The best time to plan is in early January when the days are cold and snowy and nothing else is going on in the garden. It is also a good time because seed can be ordered in plenty of time and the chances are high that you will get exactly the seed you want.

A number of tools are necessary for garden planning. First of all, a large table or other large work area to spread out on is imperative. Gather up a few gardening books (including this one) that discuss vegetables and their culture (see Suggested Reading). A stack of current seed catalogs is another necessity. Finally, graph paper, a notebook, a couple of sharp pencils, a big eraser and a ruler will round out the planning tool shed. Popcorn and mulled wine or cider are optional.

To begin, map the perimeters of the garden and the perimeters of the beds on the graph paper. Graph paper is better than regular paper because it helps to give a fairly accurate measurement of the space available, so that when planting time arrives, you won't find that you've planned to put too much in too little space. I prefer graph paper that has 10 squares to the inch, and I let each square represent six inches.

After the perimeters are set, list in the notebook all of the things you want to grow. Then go through the catalogs and choose individual varieties of the specific vegetables. This is probably the most time-consuming part of the planning process because there are so many varieites to choose from. The varieties of certain vegetables that I've found to do well in the high desert will be listed in the next chapter. For now, there are still a few things to keep in mind while you are choosing.

It's frustrating when nearly an entire crop of some vegetable ripens all at once. For two weeks, there may be tons of corn, let's say, and then for the rest of the season, nothing. To avoid innundation and disappointment, a method called successive (or staggered) planting can be employed. This technique ensures that the harvest will be staggered over a period of a month or even more, depending on the vegetable.

There are two ways to plant successively. For a steady supply of corn, for instance, varieties that ripen at different times can be planted. There are extra early varieties that are ready to eat in 65 days, while other varieties mature in 85 days from planting. And there are mid-season varieties that ripen somewhere in between the earliest and the latest types. For a staggered harvest, you might want to choose an early variety, a mid-season variety and late variety, if your growing season allows it. This type of successive planting works when there are varieties of a vegetable with a wide range of maturity dates. Such vegetables include cabbage, eggplant, melons, peas, peppers and tomatoes, although tomatoes are somewhat of a different story because early varieties are the ony ones suited to the high desert. Yet there is a variation of harvest dates even among the early types.

Another way to plant successively is to stagger the plantings. This is effective where there aren't large differences in days to maturity. To stagger plantings of lettuce, for example, simply plant short rows or small blocks of it once a week for a few weeks. That will help prevent a virtual flood of lettuce that only a rabbit could appreciate. Other vegetables that are good to stagger are snap beans, lima beans, beets, carrots, corn (if you only wish to grow one variety), cucumbers, radishes, summer squash, spinach, Swiss chard and turnips.

Another thing to watch for when choosing varieties is disease resistance. Because of the dry climate, the high desert doesn't have severe problems with plant bacterial disease, but there's no harm in choosing varieties resistant to yellows, verticillium wilt and fusarium wilt. They taste just as good as non-resistant varieties. Some varieties are resistant to pests such as nematodes, corn earworms and borers of many types. If you know of specific pests or disease problems in your area, try to choose resistant varieties.

When the varieties are finally chosen, invent an abbreviation for each one and write it beside the full name in the notebook. The abbreviation makes notations on the plan easier. For instance, I use "CK" for slicing cucumbers and "CP" for pickling cucumbers. If you plan to plant more than one variety of the same vegetable, invent an abbreviation for each variety. This may sound complicated, but as long as it's all in the

notebook, there's no chance for confusion.

Now that the varieties have been chosen and listed, it's time to put them in the plan. If you are planting in beds, simply mark off blocks and label them with the vegetable that will be planted there. By conferring with the gardening books or seed catalogs, you will know how many plants you'll be able to fit in a certain amount of space. For example, bush beans can be planted four inches apart in a raised bed, so you will be able to estimate how many plants will grow in a 15-square-foot area. In cases where vegetables are planted in "hills," like squash, it's easy just to place the abbreviation over a dot where the hill will go.

When planning a standard row garden, the first thing to do is mark the path. It is most convenient to have a 2-foot or 3-foot path down the middle. Since most of the crops will be planted in rows, it is easy to mark their location with lines that are labeled with the crop's abbreviation. For crops planted in hills, the instructions are the same as in the raised-bed garden. Mark the hill with a dot and label it.

Planning a garden makes it easy to include companion planting methods. Companion planting is a relatively new concept that puts mutually beneficial plants, vegetables and herbs together, while keeping antagonists apart. The ancient Southwestern Indians participated in companion planting without having a name for it. Corn and beans are companion plants. Beans add nitrogen to the soil and that helps the nitrogen-hungry corn, while corn provides support for pole beans and shelter from

44

high winds.

Then there are the antagonistic plants; they'd rather feud than live happily side by side. When I was a novice gardener, before the concept of companion planting was widespread, I planted beans and onions next to each other. Neither crop performed well because, it turned out, they are antagonistic and should be planted far away from each other.

Other kinds of companion plants are herbs. Certain herbs help protect certain vegetables from insect attacks. Thyme, marjoram, savory and dill, for instance, all repel the cabbage butterfly from members of the cabbage family. Companion herbs also help to improve the flavor and health of the vegetables they are compatible with.

Still another companion plant is the marigold. The French marigold, Tagetes patule, is known to repel nematodes, serious root pests. The American marigold, Tagetes erecta, repels many bugs with its pungent odor. And the American marigold also attracts many potential pests, sacrificing some of its leaves and flowers so that the vegetables will be spared. This type of protection is called trap-cropping. The French marigold is petite and easy to fit into the smallest gardens, the American marigold is tall. Both types add color to the garden.

## VEGETABLES AND THEIR COMPANIONS AND ANTAGONISTS

| Vegetable | Companion | Antagonist |
|---|---|---|
| Asparagus: | tomatoes | |
| Bush beans: | cabbage, carrots, cauliflower, corn, cucumbers, savory, potatoes | all members of the onion family |
| Beets: | carrots, kohlrabi, lettuce, onion family | pole beans |
| Cabbage family: (kale, broccoli, Brussels sprouts, cabbage, cauliflower, kohlrabi) | thyme, marjoram, savory, dill, potatoes, onions, beets | pole beans, tomatoes |
| Carrots: | lettuce, peas, onion family, tomatoes | dill |
| Celery: | bush beans, cabbage cauliflower, leeks, tomatoes | |
| Corn: | beans, cucumbers, potatoes, all types of squash | |

| Vegetable | Companion | Antagonist |
|---|---|---|
| Cucumbers | beans, corn, peas, radishes | potatoes, thyme, savory, marjoram |
| Eggplant: | beans | |
| Lettuce: | carrots, radishes | |
| Melons: | corn, nasturtiums, radishes | potatoes |
| Onion family: (chives, garlic, leek, onion, shallot) | beets, carrots, tomatoes | beans, peas |
| Peas: | carrots, corn, cucumbers, radishes | potatoes, onion family |
| Pole Beans: | cabbage, carrots, cauliflower, corn, cucumbers, summer savory, potatoes | onion family kohlrabi, sun-flowers |
| Potatoes: | beans, cabbage, corn | cucumbers, all squash, sunflowers tomatoes |
| Spinach: | strawberries | |
| Squash (including pumpkins): | corn, nasturtiums radishes | |
| Tomatoes | asparagus, basil, carrots, nasturtiums, onion, parsley | |

It is virtually impossible to get all companion plants next to each other, but try to combine companions as often as possible. In my corn patch, for example, I like to break up blocks of corn with small blocks of beans, or I plant cucumbers among the corn to shade them from the sun. This makes them somewhat difficult to find, so I prefer to plant cukes in the bed north of the corn for shading benefits. I often edge the pea patch with carrots and interplant radishes in the lettuce patch. Until it becomes second nature, all of this companion planting will be hard to keep track of, so write down companion planting notes on the margins of the plan or in the notebook. And be sure to keep antagonists well apart; just like an estrang-ed couple, they sleep in separate beds.

Crop rotation is another consideration when planning the garden. This technique is a key to the health of both the soil and the plants. The same crop should never be grown in the same place two years in a row because it tires out the soil and provides ideal conditions for the pests and diseases particular to that specific crop.

Each crop has its special demands, but they can be lumped into general categories according to those demands. Corn, for example, uses large amounts of soil nutrients, especially nitrogen. Other vegetables also classified as heavy nutrient users include asparagus, broccoli, Brussels sprouts, cabbage, cauliflower, celery, cucumbers, eggplant, kale, leeks, lettuce, melons, onions, peppers, spinach, all squash, Swiss chard, sunflowers and tomatoes.

Some vegetables do not require large quantities of nutrients. These light users are beets, carrots, garlic, kohlrabi, parsnips, potatoes (Irish and sweet), radishes and turnips.

Legumes are a special case. Because of the symbiotic relationship with microorganisms of the genus Rhizobia, legumes add nitrogen to the soil and take very little of any nutrient away. Peas and all types of beans are the most common legumes grown in the garden. We've already seen how legumes such as alfalfa and clover can be employed as green manure crops.

The idea behind crop rotation is to vary crops so that the soil is given regular rest and rejuvenation. This means, for example, that heavy users should not be planted consecutively in the same place. A good rotation schedule, starting with a well-enriched soil, could go from a heavy user to a light user to a legume and then back to a heavy user. Alternately, the rotation could be from a heavy user to a legume to a light user and back to a heavy user.

Naturally, at the beginning of every season, the soil should be fertilized and improved, and crop rotation should not be used to replace such basic maintenance. However, there are times when an area of the garden is freed in the middle of the growing season. The gardener may want to get double use of the area, especially if the garden is small. If lettuce grew there in the spring, the gardener would want to follow it with a light user like beets. On the other hand, a heavy user, such as Brussels sprouts or cauliflower, would be good to plant where spring peas grew.

When planning for members of the cabbage family, an extra consideration must be included. This family, often referred to as the Brassicas, is susceptible to a fungal disease called clubroot. To avoid clubroot, NEVER plant any Brassica in the same place more than once every three years.

One of the most puzzling parts of garden planning is deciding how much to grow of what crops. Some people garden only to have fresh produce during the growing season. Others garden in order to have enough produce to freeze and can for winter use. Either way, it's difficult to know just how much of each vegetable should be grown.

Consider the eating habits of the people you intend to feed. Does everyone consume, on the average, one carrot per day or one carrot per week? Can the household consume five pounds of squash per week or only two? How much salad does the household consume daily? How much chili does the family eat in a year?

Another good rule of thumb is to plan to grow plenty of the vegetables your family likes the best. And grow the vegetables that you consider versatile. The more ways a vegetable can be prepared, the less chance there is of everyone getting fed up with it. You know what you and your family like, so grow it. If you grow too much, give it away or preserve it in some way. If you grow too little, use the garden plan to figure out how much more to grow the next time.

# VEGETABLES AND THEIR CULTURE IN THE HIGH DESERT X

There are plenty of gardening books that thoroughly discuss the culture of common and not-so-common vegetables. This chapter is not intended to be an addition to that long list. In keeping with the theme of the book, the present chapter will discuss the common garden vegetables and their culture as it relates to high desert conditions. This list will include muskmelons and watermelons since they are so often included in the backyard garden.

Before getting on to the actual list of vegetables, it's necessary to go over a few of the basic techniques of sowing seeds.

Planting seeds is easy. The first step is to prepare the seed bed. Using a hand cultivator, chop the top two inches of soil until it is very fine and level the bed. In the case of raised beds, shape the bed into a gently sloping mound.

Whether you are planting a standard row garden or a raised-bed garden, the easiest way to sow the seeds is in rows. To make furrows for row planting, simply make narrow, straight furrows with your finger or the tip of a trowel. Under normal circumstances, the depth of the furrow should be the depth at which the seed is supposed to be planted. In the case of the high desert, the furrows should be slightly deeper than the seed is to be planted. If, for example, the seeds are supposed to be sown one-half-inch deep, make the furrow three-quarters to one-inch deep, sow the seeds and cover them with their half-inch of soil. This leaves the furrow slightly lower than the seed bed's surface which will help the furrow to collect moisture and to stay moist in spite of the drying winds that often come at planting time. This type of furrow can also be mulched with a thin layer of straw and the straw will be less apt to blow away.

For a straight row, first mark it with a piece of string whose two ends are tied to small sticks. This gardener's version of a mason's line will quickly show you whether the row is straight. In a standard row garden, the lines should be left as row markers so the gardener knows where to walk. A lot of people don't worry too much about straight rows, myself included. It's too much trouble, and in a raised-bed garden, markers aren't needed. Plants don't grow any better in straight lines than they do in slanted ones. However, where space is at a premium, the value of row markers is high.

In raised beds, the nutrients are concentrated in the bed area, so plants can be grown closer together than they are in a conventional garden. A

planting technique that fits the most plants possible into a certain area is called equidistant planting.

Let's say that bush beans are going to be planted equidistantly. In a raised bed, bush beans can be planted four inches apart. Start at the edge of the area planned for the beans, make a furrow at the proper depth and plant a bean every four inches. Make the next furrow four inches from the first one. This time, sow the first bean seed so that it is at a point halfway between the first two seeds in the first furrow. If done correctly, an imaginary triangle can be drawn with the three seeds being the three points. Continue planting the seeds four inches apart in the second furrow. In the third furrow, continue the staggered pattern, starting the first seed in line with the first seed in the first row. After all the furrows have been sown, cover them.

Beans are easy to plant equidistantly because they're so large. Smaller seeds, like lettuce, need different handling. Instead of making furrows, make small holes a little deeper than the seeds should be planted. Lettuce seed is usually planted one-quarter inch deep, so the hole should be slightly deeper. The holes should be spaced equidistantly, like the bean seeds. In the case of lettuce, the holes can be spaced four inches apart, equidistantly. Sprinkle three or four seeds in each hole and cover with one-quarter-inch of soil. The slight depressions will collect water and after the seeds have germinated, they will have to be thinned so that only one plant is growing at each spot.

A slightly simpler method of planting that doesn't fit quite as many plants in an area is what I call grid planting. Imagine that the area where the beans are going to grow is a checkerboard made of four-inch squares. Plant a seed in the middle of each imaginary square and all of the plants will be four inches from each other in every direction. The checkerboard can be drawn in directly on the seed bed.

The equidistant technique and the grid technique also work when transplanting seedlings. These techniques take a bit of getting used to, so it may be advantageous to plant a few crops using a new technique and plant others in standard rows.

When sowing seeds in rows, sow the seed sparingly. This is especially important for tiny seeds like carrots and lettuce. The thicker the seed is sown, the more thinning will have to be done. Thinning is a necessary chore that is rather heartbreaking. But if seedlings are allowed to grow too close together, they never develop into robust plants.

Thin seedlings after they've put on one or two true leaves. Thinning can be done gradually, especially for lettuce, spinach and carrots. For instance, carrots should be thinned to eventually stand about three inches apart. Start by thinning them to stand one-half inch apart. In a week to ten days, thin again so that they stand an inch apart. When they start to crowd each other, thin again, and again, until they are at the correct spacing. The thinnings can be used in salads. I realize that it is hard to pull up tiny, defenseless plants, but it must be done, so gather your resolve, get on your hands and knees and do it!

Before you thin, of course, you have to make sure the seeds germinate. After the seed is sown and the soil tamped gently but firmly with the palm of the hand, water the seed bed well with a light mist. Spraying too hard will compact the soil and it might even wash away the smaller seeds. It is best to sow seed in soil that's already damp. This is particularly important in the high desert because the soil in the spring can be bone dry. A few weeks before planting time, run the irrigation system once or twice a week to add moisture to the soil. And, after the seeds are planted, it is frequently necessary to water the seed beds two and three times a day because the dry spring winds can dehydrate one-half inch of soil in a couple of hours.

Some vegetables do not mature fast enough to be sown directly into the garden. The weather gets too hot before spring crops of broccoli, cauliflower and cabbage can mature. For other vegetables, like peppers and tomatoes, the frost-free season isn't long enough to mature their fruit. These plants are best started indoors, weeks before they are to be transplanted into the garden. Plants that have very tiny seeds, such as thyme and oregano, are best started indoors, too.

Many people think it is too difficult to raise their own seedlings, so they purchase them at planting time from a local nursery. For some reason, most nurseries in the high desert carry only a limited number of varieties, many of which aren't suited to the high desert climate. So there is a real advantage to raising your own seedlings. You get a choice!

Thanks to the high desert's sunny winters, a south-facing windowsill is all that's really needed to grow seedlings indoors. Depending on the amount of plants you're growing, paper cups, styrofoam cups, milk cartons, peat pots and wooden flats are all suitable containers for starting seeds. I grow at least one hundred seedlings of various vegetables for my garden, so flats suit my purposes the best. For a gardener who plans on a dozen seedlings, paper cups are much more convenient and much less expensive. Peat pots are often used to start seedlings. They are nothing more than compressed peat moss (some have built-in fertilizers) and plants grown in them can be transplanted, pot and all, right into the garden. Peat pots dry out very quickly, so they must be monitored closely.

It is imperative that a sterile growing medium is used for starting seed indoors. Regular garden soil contains pathogens that love the conditions of indoor seed flats. The best growing medium is a mixture of one-part sphagnum peat moss and one-part vermiculite or perlite — unusual minerals with excellent water-holding capacities.

To sterilize your own mix, pour boiling water through the mixture, making sure that all parts get wet. There are excellent, pre-sterilized growing mediums on the market. These mixtures are one of the few prepackaged gardening products I purchase.

When planting the seeds, plant more than you'll actually need. Put two or three seeds in each individual pot and eventually thin them so only the most robust plant remains. In flats, sow more than you'll need and eventually thin the seedlings to stand two inches apart. Don't forget to label all containers. Many seedlings, especially those of the cabbage family, look alike to the inexperienced eye.

It is best to use a sprayer or mister of some sort to water the seed flats. This provides a gentle mist that won't wash the soil off the seeds. Misting is especially effective for watering very fine seed that is barely covered with soil. Use water that is room temperature or slightly warmer. Never use cold or hot water.

Most seeds prefer temperatures between 60 and 70 degrees F. for germination. Some seeds, such as those of the cabbage family, will germinate at temperatures as low as 55 degrees, while other seeds, notably eggplants, peppers and tomatoes, prefer a steady 75 degrees for their best germination. In cool houses, it may be necessary to start seeds on top of the refrigerator or freezer, or in some other warm spot. After the seeds have sprouted, move them to the windowsill.

When the seedlings put on their first set of true leaves, start feeding them. The first set of leaves to emerge are the cotyledons, which are not true leaves. The second set will be the true leaves. A fish emulsion fertilizer gives the best results, but if there is a cat in the house it is probably wiser to use a mild synthetic houseplant fertilizer. In either case, feed the seedlings once a week to keep them healthy. As they grow, the plants may develop a list in the direction of the major light source. To keep the seedlings growing straight, turn the containers at least once a week.

When to start seeds indoors depends on the variety. In general, most seeds are planted indoors six to eight weeks before they are to be transplanted. Frost-tender vegetables should be planted six to eight weeks before the last-frost date. Vegetables that can be transplanted before the frost-free date, such as broccoli and cabbage, should be started four to six weeks before their planting date. Consult the seed packet or the seed catalog for specific information. For an effective reminder, mark indoor and outdoor planting dates on your calendar.

At this point let me clarify just what the last-frost date and the first-frost date are. The last-frost date (or the frost-free date) is the average day on which the latest frost of the spring occurs. The first-frost date is the average day when the first frost of the fall season can be expected. These dates are ONLY averages and should NEVER be taken as law. Frosts sometimes occur after the last-frost date and before the first-frost date, so one should not depend on average dates alone. Instead, pay special attention to the weather at all times, especially within two weeks of the last-frost date and the first-frost date. Use you own observations coupled with information from a reliable weather service. After a couple of seasons, you will begin to know what the night air feels like when a frost is likely and what kind of weather patterns bring cold or warm air.

Most areas of the high desert have between 100 and 120 frost-free days, except for the high mountain valleys, where the frost-free seasons can be 80 days, or even shorter. For the official frost dates for your area, consult the county agricultural extension agent that is provided by the land-grant university of your state.

About a week before transplanting time, the seedlings should be hardened off. This process is to toughen them up for life in the great outdoors. Start by moving seedlings outside in the mid-morning or early afternoon. The temperature must be above freezing. Give the seedlings no more than an hour of sun the first day out, keep them sheltered from the wind and after the first hour, move them to a shady spot. Each day step up the amount of sunshine they receive, and give them a slight taste of the wind. A few minutes of wind goes a long way toward toughening the seedlings' stems. While they are outside, keep a close watch on the their water supply; do not let them dry out.

If the seedlings are sharing a flat, start the hardening off process by cutting a two-inch-by-two-inch square around each seedling with a sharp knife. This may sound radical but it will stimulate the growth of tiny root hairs and will prevent undue shock at transplanting time, when it's more difficult to recover. After cutting, water the flats well and move them to a shady area inside the house. When the plants have recovered from their shock (about two days), they can start the hardening off process described above.

Transplanting is an easy but time-consuming chore. Dig a hole that is larger than the root ball of the seedling. In soil that isn't well enriched, such as in a first-year garden, it is a good practice to dig a hole six to nine inches deep, place a trowelful of compost and some bone meal in the bottom of the hole, cover that with a thin layer of soil and then transplant the seedling. Never plant the seedling directly in manure or compost.

Always plant the seedling slightly lower in the garden than it was growing in its container. When handling the seedling, avoid holding it by its stem, which is tender and easily bruised. The best way to hold a seedling is by cupping a hand gently below and around the leaves. If the root ball is too heavy for this kind of handling, hold the plant gingerly by its root ball. Do not remove the seedling from its container until its hole is ready and, when using peat pots, be sure that they are very wet, almost soggy, when they are planted.

After the seedling is planted, tamp the soil firmly and create a small trough around each plant. Into the trough pour a fish emulsion solution or manure tea to help the plant get off to a good start. Usually one half of a one-pound coffee can is plenty for each seedling.

After the fertilizer has soaked in, a cutworm collar must be placed around each plant. Cutworms will chew tender seedlings at the point where the stem meets the soil until the plant topples over. A collar made of stiff paper helps to foil the cutworm's dirty deed. I prefer the cardboard that is used in six-pack cartons. It is sturdy, yet pliable and easy to find.

To make a cutworm collar, cut the cardboard into strips that are almost one and one-half inches wide and seven inches long. Place the strip so it encircles the plant stem without touching it, and push the collar gently into the soil so that half of the strip is below the soil. This works in most cases.

The best time to transplant is on an overcast day, but those are rare in the high desert spring. Try to transplant in the late afternoon to avoid the rays of the midday sun. If you have lots and lots of seedlings, you will probably have to start in the morning, or if you have the time, you can spread the planting over a few afternoons. If you have only a few seedlings, you can protect them from the sun with individual tents fashioned out of a folded sheet of newspaper. Weight the tents down with stones or soil and leave them on for three or four days. If the seedlings have been hardened off properly, they probably won't require much protection from the sun and wind.

## A GUIDE TO GROWING COMMON GARDEN VEGETABLES IN THE HIGH DESERT

### Asparagus / Liliaceae

Asparagus is a big spring favorite and an excellent vegetable for the high desert garden. It is a perennial and if properly handled while it is establishing, an asparagus bed will produce well for upwards of 25 years. I have often run across asparagus growing in high desert fields where farms and homes once stood.

All varieties of asparagus do well in the high desert, so choose one that is disease resistant. Asparagus is planted by crowns (dormant, 2-year-old seedlings) in a permanent bed and cannot be harvested until the third spring after planting. The stalks grow into tall, fernlike plants, so the bed should be situated on the north side of the garden where it won't limit other plantings by making an area too shady. Because of its permanent postition and its love for a steady supply of water, asparagus is well-suited to drip irrigation. It is somewhat drought-hardy but does not do well during prolonged dry spells.

### Beans / Leguminosae

Beans are a traditional food of the Southwest and were a staple of ancient Indians, including the Aztec and Maya. The most famous bean in the Southwestern United States is the pinto bean and rightfully so for it grows very well in the high desert climate. Other dried beans, such as black beans and navy beans, as well as string (or snap) beans, also do well here. The *Bolita* (or *Boleta*) bean is related to the pinto and is especially adapted to the short season areas of the high mountains. The *Tepari* bean was domesticated by the Papago Indians in the low desert and is very drought and heat tolerant. It is best suited to warm areas of the high desert.

Though most beans are frost-tender, the *Fava* or broadbean (Vicia faba) can be planted as soon as the soil can be worked in the spring. It thrives on cool weather and was grown by the early Spanish settlers in the coldest areas of the high desert. Some people are allergic to fava beans.

Beans seem to be the most sensitive plants in the vegetable garden when it comes to iron deficiency (chlorosis). When the pH rises too high and iron is made unavailable to plants, beans will show the deficiency first. Their leaves will turn bright yellow but the veins will stay dark green. Be sure to add lots of good compost and some cottonseed meal to the bean patch in a first-year garden. The pH will probably be under control by the second year. If the beans develop chlorosis despite precautions, side dress with ferrous sulfate. It may be necessary to do so once a week. *Roma*, the tasty Italian string bean, seems to be most sensitive to the iron problem. Pole beans (the ones that climb) are the next most susceptible type.

### Beets / Chenopodiaceae

All beets grow well in the high desert as long as they have a steady supply of water. Cover the beds with a thick layer of straw (at least 12 inches thick) sometime after the first hard frost. This will enable you to continue harvesting at least through Thanksgiving.

## Broccoli / Cruciferae

The high desert is broccoli country. The cool nights of summer produce some of the finest fall crops of broccoli you'll ever taste and the spring crops are good, too. Broccoli can be transplanted into the garden four weeks before the last frost date. It can also be sown directly in the garden in early June for a fall harvest. When direct-seeding in June, keep the seed bed covered with a light mulch to keep the seeds cool and moist. When the summer rains come, the broccoli will really take off!

## Brussels Sprouts / Cruciferae

Brussels sprouts are planted in mid-spring for a fall harvest. They grow well in the high desert summers, thriving on the cool nighttime temperatures and afternoon thunderstorms. The seeds can be sown in late May or early June directly into the garden or they can be started indoors in a cool place in mid-to-late May and then transplanted into the garden when the seedlings are four weeks old.

Brussels sprouts taste best when they've been nipped by frost and they get better as the weather gets colder. In good years, the sprouts can be harvested well in to December.

## Cabbage / Cruciferae

Cabbage is yet another Brassica that thrives in the high desert if it is given a good supply of water. Plant early varieties for late spring crops, mid-season varieties for summer crops and late varieties for fall harvest and storage. *Earliana, Early Jersey Wakefield* and *Golden Acre* are excellent early types; *All Seasons Wisconsin, Copenhagen Market, Savoy Age* and *Superpack* are good mid-season varieties; and *Danish Roundhead* and *Late Danish* are good fall varieties. Don't fail to grow red cabbage, the most popular variety being *Ruby Ball Hybrid.*

## Carrots / Umbelliferae

The carrot is a good vegetable for high desert gardens, especially in raised beds where they grow long and straight. Carrot seed is naturally slow to germinate and it is particularly slow in high desert springs because the soil dries so quickly. Although instructions say to plant seed one-quarter-inch deep, planting them one-half inch deep will help them stay moist and will not prevent germination. Plantings later in the season germinate better.

Stagger plantings from early April through the end of July. Cover the seed beds with a light mulch to help retain moisture. In the fall, when the tops die back, cover the bed with a layer of straw at least 12 inches thick and continue to harvest carrots well into December, if not for the entire winter.

The best long carrots are considered to be the many *Nantes* varieties, such as *Nantes Coreless, Nantes Fancy, Nantes Half Longs* and *Nantes Strong Top*. In heavy soils it is wise to plant the short, stubbier carrots that are just as sweet as the long types. These short varieties include *Kundulus, Oxheart, Red-Cored Chantenay, Royal Chantenay* and *Short 'n' Sweet*. If you are a fan of baby carrots, you'll be disappointed with the flavor of young, standard carrots. For the best tasting "baby" carrots, grow *Carrot Sucram*, a miniature carrot with a fine, sweet flavor.

### Cauliflower / Cruciferae
Cauliflower is best grown as a fall crop in the high desert. The plants can be started by directly sowing the seed in the garden in early June, or seedlings can be started indoors in a cool place in mid-May for transplanting in late June. Be sure to spread a light mulch over the seed bed to keep it moist and cool. Choose varieties that will mature in 50 to 65 days, before the first frost, as cauliflower is one of the few Brassicas that is frost-tender. Remember that harvest dates are calculated from the time the seedling is set out, so if you are direct-seeding, add 28 days to the printed harvest date.

### Celery / Umbelliferae
Celery is a water-loving plant. It is best planted by a leaky faucet or in an area where water collects. If using a drip system, the celery will require a few extra emitters. Homegrown celery is tasty, but the amount of water it requires makes this vegetable less than ideal for the high desert vegetable garden.

### Chinese Cabbage / Cruciferae
Like standard cabbages, Chinese cabbage and all of its relatives are excellent vegetables for the high desert garden. They are good for both spring and fall crops. Of the heading, nappa-type cabbage, *Michili* and *Two Season's Hybrid* are highly recommended. Of the non-heading, pakchoi types, the variety *Pak Choy* or *Bok Choy* is recommended for the home garden. Both the nappa types and the pakchoi types can be grown as spring and fall crops.

### Corn / Gramineae
Corn is a native of the New World and there is evidence that it existed in Mexico 5,000 years ago. Corn was the foundation of the great civilizations of the Aztecs and the Mayas as well as being a staple of the ancient Indians of the Southwestern United States. Raising corn in the backyard garden is participating in a tradition.

Because it is native to this part of the world, corn has few problems in the high desert. In the very short season of the high mountain valleys, corn used to be an "iffy" crop, but today's quick maturing hybrids have solved that problem; most mature within 70 to 80 days.

There is usually no need to start corn indoors and it doesn't transplant very well. In some very short season areas, planting indoors can be tried. To reduce the risk of severe transplant shock, grow corn seedlings in their own individual containers. Planting instructions often say to plant seed in hills. Water rolls off hills, so it is better to plant them in slight depressions that will catch the water. In raised beds, corn can be planted equidistantly, a few seeds to each depression. Thin plants later so that only the healthiest plant of each group remains. In conventional row gardens, do not plant corn in a single row. Pollination is vital to kernel formation, so corn should be planted in blocks at least four rows wide to ensure pollination.

Most people grow sweet corn for on-the-cob eating and for freezing. If there is room in the garden, it's worth planting a few seeds of blue corn, one of the original corn varieties. The kernels are blue-black and are allowed to mature and dry before they're harvested. Many people prize blue corn meal, and blue corn tortillas are particularly appreciated thoughout the Southwestern United States for their rich flavor.

### Cucumbers / Cucurbitaceae

What would summer be without cucumbers? This cooling and versatile vegetable gets off to a slow start in the high desert due to the intense heat and sunshine that usually comes in the month of June. For better early growth, plant the cukes where they will receive some shade, or shade the young plants with bushel baskets. Don't forget to mulch as soon as the soil warms up; cucumbers are shallow-rooted and need a steady supply of moisture.

In limited space, cukes can be trained up trellises or fences, or the new bush-type, space-saving varieties can be grown. Try the delicious *Lemon* cucumber. It is round and yellow, and tends to be sweeter than regular cucumbers.

### Eggplant / Solanaceae

Eggplant can be a real heartbreaker in the high desert. It is a heat-lover and it will sit in the garden and wait for the weather to get hot. When the weather finally heats up, the cool nights will continue to slow the eggplant down. The standard eggplant, *Black Beauty*, will sometimes produce a satisfactory harvest, but for a better chance at a good crop, try *Dusky Hybrid* (65 days), *Early Hybrid* (62 days) or the Japanese eggplant, *Ichiban* (61 days). In mountain valleys where summer nighttime temperatures rarely push out of the low 50s, eggplant may not be feasible at all.

## Garlic / Amaryllidaceae

Garlic is easily grown and can often become an irritating weed. Start garlic from individual cloves, planting in early spring for a fall harvest or in early fall for a harvest of very full bulbs in the following fall. Fall planting usually yields the best results for me.

Because the cloves are so simple to handle, garlic can easily be planted thoughout the garden as a bug repellant plant. Remember to keep garlic, and all other members of the onion family, away from peas and beans.

## Kale / Cruciferae

Kale is an oft-neglected and unfairly maligned green that is extremely cold hardy. It is often harvested well past Thanksgiving and tastes best after a few hard frosts. Like other Brassicas, kale enjoys the high desert's cool nights and can be raised as a spring crop, but the best crop comes in the fall.

## Kohlrabi / Cruciferae

Kohlrabi seems to be a "fad" vegetable. Americans go "mad" for it every so often after which it fades back into an uneasy obscurity. Kohlrabi is delicious steamed, deep-fried and raw. It can be started indoors in the spring and transplanted outside three to four weeks before the last frost date, or it can be sown directly into the garden in early spring. The best tasting crop of kohlrabi comes in the fall from seeds sown in June through mid-July.

## Leeks / Amaryllidaceae

This easy-to-grow member of the onion family is the crucial ingredient in an authentic vichyssoise and it makes all soups and stews taste wonderful. Milder than onions, leeks are quite expensive in the stores, so they are well worth growing in the garden, especially since they take up little space.

Start seeds indoors so that they are six weeks old when transplanted at three to four weeks before the last frost date. Plant the seedlings in a trench and, as they grow, mound soil around them so the stalks will blanch. The white part of the stalk is definitely the tastiest.

If they are heavily mulched, leeks can be harvested in all but the coldest months of the winter, and then again in the early spring.

## Lettuce / Compositae

Lettuce is simple to grow and is a very good crop for the high desert. Lettuce can be sown directly in the garden about four weeks before the last frost date in the spring, and successive planting can be made every 10 days or so until two weeks after the last frost date. Because high desert nights

60

are cool, lettuce often stands until the end of July before it goes to seed.

Avoid the iceberg types that require long periods of wet, cool weather. Do try the Bibb types and the non-heading varieties. *Prizehead, Oak Leaf* and *Salad Bowl* are three excellent non-heading lettuces.

## Melon / Cucurbitaceae

Although melons are thought of as a sweet fruit, they are grown in the vegetable garden, so they are included in this list. There is a strange notion that cantaloupe and honeydew melons do not produce well in the high desert. This idea must be based on myth because many high desert gardeners regularly harvest good crops of melons.

The trick to melon culture in the high desert is to grow early-maturing varieties in a well-drained, warm soil. Melons will tolerate a pH from 6.0 to 8.0, so that is not a problem, but the soil should be generously enriched with compost or rotted manure.

Another trick for melons is to start them indoors, no earlier than four weeks before the last-frost date. Start seeds in individual containers such as small pots, peat pots or paper cups, so that the seedling can be popped out of the container and into the garden with a minimum of disturbance. Plant the seedlings in hills, three to a hill, or seeds can be sown six to a hill and thinned later to the three healthiest plants. Although it is hard to keep hills moist in the high desert, the soil warms up faster in hills and warm soil is crucial to success with melons. Black plastic can be used as a mulch to retain moisture and help the soil warm. Once the plants start vining, the plastic can be removed and saved for use at another time.

Early varieties of muskmelons include *Burpee's Ambrosia Hybrid* (86 days), *Burpee Hybrid* (82 days), *Delicious* (85 days), *Earlisweet* (79 days), *Early and Sweet* (85 days), *Far North* (65 days, small fruits), *Harper Hybrid* (86 days), *Short 'n' Sweet* (75 days), *Sweet Granite* (75 days), and *Sweet 'n' Early Hybrid* (75 days, small fruits).

Early varieties of honeydews include *Earlidew* (85 days), *Honey Drip* Hybrid (85 days) and *Park's Pineapple Hybrid* (85 days).

## Okra / Malvaceae

Okra is another much-maligned vegetable, yet it is an essential ingredient in Creole cooking, especially in gumbos. Okra is also delicious fried. Though okra prefers the heat and humidity of the southeastern United States, it will produce a good crop in the high desert. It tolerates soils that are slightly alkaline and actually prefers a dry soil.

## Onions / Amaryllidaceae

Onions are so inexpensive and they keep so well in a cool place, many people with small gardens don't see any need to grow them. However, always set some space aside for a steady supply of scallions. Large red onions, pure white onions and pearl onions (a gourmet treat) can all be quite expensive, so it might be worthwhile to include a few in any garden. In all cases, onions are a great high desert crop, although the shorter-season areas may have a difficult time getting large-size bulbs.

Onions can be started from seed indoors so that they are six weeks old when transplanted into the garden at four weeks before the last frost date. A good crop is close to a sure thing with sets but they are relatively expensive and varieties available in sets are limited. Growing onions from seedlings yields the best results and seeds offer a better selection of varieties, especially the early types.

### Peas / Leguminosae

Peas are a spring and fall crop, and they usually produce good harvest in the high desert. Certainly, there is nothing that equals the taste of peas from the garden, and for Oriental food enthusiasts, the only way to have a good, inexpensive supply of snow peas is to grow them.

Peas are the first vegetable planted in the spring; in mid- to late-March on the lower elevations and in April in the higher elevations. Make sure the seed beds are well supplied with moisture and be patient, for the seeds may take up to three weeks to germinate while they wait for the soil temperature to be just right. Innoculate peas with the nitrogen-fixing bacteria that helps them grow if peas have never grown in the area where they're being planted. This legume innoculant is available from seed catalogs. Some planting instructions recommend soakng the seed for 24 hours before planting but this practice tends to cause the seeds to rot instead of sprout. For a fall harvest, plant peas in mid-July or at least 65 days before the first-frost date.

Do try *Sugar Snap*, an edible-pod pea that is at its best when the peas are large and the pods swollen. They are delicious raw in salads or as hors d'ouvres. There are now dwarf varieties of this pea, which has become America's favorite. *Little Marvel* is an early, dependable and prolific shell pea that does not require trellising. *Mammoth Melting Sugar* is the most popular snow pea and the *Dwarf Gray Sugar* is a snow pea that doesn't need trellising.

### Peppers, Hot / Solanaceae

There are so many varieties of hot peppers, it is difficult for the spicy-food aficionado not to fill half the garden with them. Luckily, all hot peppers are very prolific, so in many cases, only one or two plants are necessary for a year's supply.

Hot peppers are excellent high desert vegetables. They aren't heavy feeders and they are rarely bothered by pests or disease. Most hot peppers mature quickly and produce fruit even in short-season areas.

Peppers are frost-tender and should be started indoors six to eight weeks before the last frost date. If you love hot peppers, growing your own seedlings is a definite advantage because many varieties of hot peppers just can't be found at nurseries.

Some gardeners decrease the amount of water hot peppers receive as the fruit is maturing in order to get extra hot peppers. This technique, called stressing, is especially well-suited to the many varieties of green chile (also known as Anaheim chile). When using this technique, be careful not to let the soil dry so much that the plants are over-stressed and weakened. Also remember that young pepper plants require a steady supply of moisture.

The numerous strains of green chile that are available differ in the quality of their fruit and the degree of their piquance. *Big Jim* produces a long, fleshy pod with a mild flavor that is excellent for stuffing. *Rio Grande* also produces a fleshy pod but it's not quite as long as *Big Jim's* and it tends to be hotter. *Sandia* is a very hot green chile that produces a long but less meaty pod. *Espanola Improved* is a new variety of green chile that was developed by New Mexico State University. *Espanola Improved* will ripen (turn red) on the vine in short-season areas. *Anaheim, Nu-Mex Big Jim* and *Chimayo* are other mild green chiles. The high desert gardener who doesn't grow at least a few green chile plants is really missing a treat.

Of course, green chiles are just at the beginning of the list of hot peppers, and the hottest of the green chiles are mild compared to most other hot peppers. Hot peppers are used around the world in all tropical areas and a wide variety of them exist. Of the milder hots, there is the ever-popular *Hungarian Yellow Wax*, a stubby yellow pepper, and the *Red Cherry Large* which is excellent for pickling. *Long Red Cayenne* is fiery hot and is good fresh or it can be dried and ground. *Jalapeno* is the stubby pepper that adds the characteristic fire to many Mexican dishes. *Ancho 101* is a dark green, wide-shouldered, Poblano-type pepper that is used fresh for stuffing. When dried, this is the chile to be used in mole, the Mexican chocolate, peanut and chile sauce. *Serrano* and *Chile Piquin* are two other hot Mexican peppers. *Habanero* is yet another hot pepper from Mexico, this one from the Yucatan Peninsula. According to Texas A&M University, the *Habanero* is one thousand times hotter than the *Jalapeno*. The hottest pepper with seeds currently available in the United States is probably the *Thai Hot Pepper*. This pepper barely reaches one inch in length and packs a lot more punch than the *Habenero*. It is essential for Oriental dishes and the plant itself is compact, decorative and suited to indoor culture.

Two other peppers that are neither hot nor bells are the *Paprika* and the *Pepperoncini*. The *Paprika* produces the famous mild red powder when it is dried and ground. The *Pepperoncini* is a mildly tangy Italian pepper found in antipastos and Greek salads. It pickles well.

All gardens should have at least one hot pepper plant, even if it's only to serve as a conversation piece.

### Peppers, Sweet / Solanaceae

Sweet (or bell) peppers are as easy to grow as hot peppers. They ripen well in the sunny high desert and produce abundant yields. There's no reason why they shouldn't be included in the garden.

Sweet peppers are a sure-fire success in a well-drained, well-enriched soil. They require a steady supply of moisture and are rarely bothered by pests or disease. Most sweet peppers start producing mature fruits within 60 to 80 days from transplanting. A mulch of light-colored straw helps the fruits to ripen quickly and evenly.

Sweet peppers should be started indoors, six to eight weeks before the last frost date. In short-season areas, early varieties should be grown. Again, this is when starting your own seedlings is advantageous; many nurseries do not sell early varieties.

In my high desert garden, I have had the best results from *Burpee's Tasty Hybrid* (70 days), *California Wonder* (75 days), *Gypsy Hybrid* (65 days), and *Staddon's Select* (65 days). *California Wonder* is the standard blocky-type bell pepper that is found in the grocery store. *Tasty Hybrid* is slightly less blocky than *California Wonder*. *Gypsy* produces an amazing amount of flavorful, yellow, tapered peppers. In the short-season areas, *Gypsy* is the best bet, but also give *Staddon's Select* and *Ace* (50 days) a try. Don't fail to allow at least a few peppers to turn red on the vine.

### Potatoes / Solanaceae

Potatoes fresh from the garden are unequalled in flavor and texture but they pose a bit of a problem in the high desert. Potatoes are prone to numerous diseases and are at their healthiest in acid soils. The best results will be obtained from a soil with a pH of 5.2 to 5.7, a range that's almost impossible to attain in the high desert. Good yields will come from a soil with a pH that runs between 6.0 and 6.5, and decent harvests can be had from a soil with a pH between 6.5 and 7.0, though the plants tend to be highly vulnerable to disease at that pH range.

The best way to lower the pH in the potato patch is to add generous amounts of compost and cottonseed meal before planting. Their acidifying effects will hopefully produce a better crop.

When planting potatoes, make sure the seed potatoes (which are nothing more than regular potato tubers) are certified to be disease-free. Do not use potatoes from the grocery store because they usually carry disease and are often treated with a growth inhibitor. Potatoes can also be grown from real seed. Start them six to eight weeks before the last frost date.

### Radishes / Cruciferae

Radishes are a never-fail crop. They are a cool-weather vegetable and should be sown successively from early April though mid-May, and again from late August through mid-September. Plant radishes among spinach, lettuce and carrots and in hills of squash and melons to repel bugs. Do try the Oriental-type radishes that grow very large and are good in salads and stir-fry.

### Rhubarb / Polygonaceae

Rhubarb is a perennial that eventually occupies 12 square feet of garden space. It is an attractive plant that would be at home in any perennial flower bed if the vegetable garden is too small to accomodate it. Rhubarb leaves are toxic but the bright red stalks (actually leaf petioles) are used to make a tart sauce or pie.

Rhubarb is very hardy in the high desert, though it does prefer a steady supply of moisture and will be very unhappy if the soil around its roots dries out. Once established, a rhubarb plant will live forever.

Rhubarb is one of the first things harvested in the spring and its fresh, tangy taste is a welcome relief from the standard winter vegetables. It is also loaded with vitamin A and potassium.

### Spinach / Chenopodiaceae

Spinach is a hardy leaf crop that performs well in high desert conditions. A cool-weather crop, spinach will often produce succulent leaves well into July in the high desert, thanks to the cool nights. Spinach can be planted successively from early April through early May (and even later in the cooler areas). Spinach likes a soil that's well enriched with rotted manure or compost, and it requires a steady supply of water. Some of the more popular varieties include *Bloomsdale Long-Standing, Avon Hybrid* and *Melody*. There are, however, many suitable varieties to choose from. Don't forget to plant a fall crop in mid-August for harvest in early October. Covered with a thick mulch, spinach can sometimes be harvested into early November.

### Squash / Cucurbitaceae

Squash is a native to the Americas and was a main part of the Amerindian diet throughout the American continents. Squash comes in many forms and flavors, from the quick-maturing, soft-skin summer types to the pumpkins and the hard-skin winter types. Because squash is native to this part of the world, it grows very well here. All types of squash can be grown throughout the high desert, except for the very short-season areas where the late winter squashes may have to be sacrificed.

Squash is an interesting crop in the high desert because there are so many local varieties that can't be found in any seed catalog. People will often offer seeds of local varieties to their gardening neighbors. Always keep eyes and ears open for unusual varieties and make sure to allow some of the fruit to mature completely so the seed can be collected and the strain perpetuated.

Squash is very frost-tender and must be planted after all danger of frost has passed. If garden space is limited, try some of the new, space-saving varieties such as *Burpee's Bush Table Queen* (acorn type), *Burpees's Butterbush* (butternut-type), *Bush Acorn Table King, Cinderella Pumpkin, Spirit Hybrid Pumpkin* and *Squash Park's Creamy Hybrid.*

### Sweet Potatoes / Convolvulaceae

The sweet potato is a relative of the morning glory, not particularly suited to the high desert, but will sometimes give satisfactory harvests. This tuber prefers long hot summers and gives its best performance where the frost-free growing season lasts 150 to 160 days. When selecting a sweet potato variety, select one that matures in 90 to 100 days, which in most cases will be *Centennial.* Sweet potatoes are planted from slips (seedlings). The slips can be started from sweet potatoes purchased at the grocery store, but you can't be sure of the variety, so it is better to order them from a reputable seed company. Sweet potatoes are grown in the warmer areas of the Southwest and are generally inexpensive, so I've often wondered whether devoting garden space to such an unreliable crop is worth the trouble.

### Swiss Chard / Chenopodiaceae

Swiss chard is a beet that produces giant leaves instead of a swollen root. It stands up to summer heat, which makes it an excellent green to replace spinach when the weather gets hot. Chard prefers a steady supply of moisture and if it is allowed to dry out, it will promptly go to seed. A thick mulch placed around it in June will protect against drying.

Harvest the outer leaves, taking a few from each plant, and the plants will continue to produce leaves throughout the summer and well past the frost. You will find that the larger leaves aren't as tasty as the small leaves, so you'll want to harvest the chard regularly before the leaves get too big.

## Tomato / Solanaceae

When people think of vegetable gardens, they think of tomatoes. And it's no wonder; a ripe tomato, fresh off the vine, is an unparalleled treat. This native of tropical America grows well in most parts of the United States, but the high desert is not particularly conducive to tomato culture. The cool summer nights retard the ripening of the fruit, so the high desert gardener usually has to resort to special varieties.

Today there are numerous tomato varieties that are designed to produce crops in the cool climates of northern New England and Canada. These varieties, believe it or not, are the ones that will produce crops in the high desert. Some of these cool climate tomatoes are *Coldset* (70 days), *Earlibright* (65 days), *Earlirouge* (69 days), *Early Cascade* (52 days), *Early Girl Hybrid* (54 days), *Heinz No. 2653* (plum-type, 68 days), *J.S.S No. 3570* (59 days), *Jackpot* (71 days), *Nova* (plum-type, 72 days), *Red Express 238* (74 days), *Small Fry Hybrid* (cherry-type, 52 days), *Springset* (67 days), *Sub-Arctic Mini* (56 days), *Sub-Arctic Plenty* (58 days), and *Whippersnapper* (cherry-type, 52 days). New varieties are introduced every year. At elevations above 8,000 feet, the earliest varieties should be planted.

If you grew up where tomatoes weighed three-fourths of a pound apiece and tasted like tomato-flavored sugar, you might as well say goodbye to them and settle for the smaller and slightly acid, cool-climate varieties. If the garden is adjacent to a south-facing wall, it might be worthwhile to experiment with mid-season varieties (75 to 80 days) planted adjacent to the wall. At night the wall will release heat it picked up during the day, thus keeping the tomatoes warmer. The only other way to get the large, longer season varieties is to grow them in a greenhouse. Other gardeners who have tried to grow tomatoes in the high desert and failed will try to discourage you from growing them. Grow a short-season variety and show them how plant geneticists have conquered the climate!

## Turnips / Cruciferae

The turnip is a double-duty vegetable because both its root and its leaves are good eating. The turnip grows well in the high desert and requires little special attention. Sow the seed successively from the beginning of April though the end of July for a constant supply of this sweet and versatile root. After the first hard freeze, cover the turnip bed with a thick layer of straw and continue to pull turnips up through Thanksgiving.

*Shogoin* is grown especially for its greens, which are loaded with vitamins. *Tokyo Cross Hybrid* is a quick-maturing turnip that's ready for the table in 35 days. It does not hold up well in warm weather, so for summer turnips, depend on one of the standard purple-top varieties.

## Watermelon / Cucurbitaceae

The watermelon is a tropical fruit and, like muskmelon, it is usually grown in the vegetable garden. With names like *Dixie Queen* and *Congo*, one would assume that watermelons like long, hot summers and this is an accurate assumption. For a successful crop of watermelons in the high desert, early-maturing, small-fruited varieties of watermelons should be grown. Though they are smaller, their taste is just sweet and juicy as the larger varieties.

Watermelons like a well-drained soil that has been generously enriched with compost and/or well-rotted manure. Start the plants indoors about four weeks before the last frost date. Plant the seeds in individual peat pots to minimize disturbance at transplanting time. Transplant the seedlings three to a hill when the soil has warmed up. A mulch of black plastic can be used to help warm the soil quickly. (See Melon listing.) I do not suggest the direct-seeding of watermelons.

Early watermelon varieties include *Burpee's Fordhook Hybrid* (74 days), *New Hampshire Midget* (70 days), *New Shipper* (75 days), *Sugar Baby* (75 days), and *Sugar Bush* (80 days, bush type, space-saving variety).

Although local nurseries sell seeds and seedlings, the only way to grow exactly what you want is to order seeds from the mail-order seed catalogs. The following is a list of the many seed companies that sell their seeds through catalogs.

One of the most famous seed companies, Burpee's offers a wide variety of seeds. Excellent selection of marigolds and vegetables.

W. Atlee Burpee Company
300 Park Avenue
Warminster, Pennsylavania 18974

Gurney's entertaining catalog lists a wide variety of seeds, including novelty vegetables and varieties for cool climates. There is a good selection of hot peppers.

Gurney's Seed and Nursery Company
Yankton, South Dakota 57079

Harris lists a lot of short-season vegetables that have been proven in trials at its farm near Rochester, N.Y.

Joseph Harris Co., Inc.
3670 Buffalo Road
Moreton Farm
Rochester, New York 14624

Herbst offers an extensive listing of vegetables and flowers.
>Herbst Brothers Seedsmen, Inc.
>1000 N. Main Street
>Brewster, New York 10509

Johnny's specializes in seeds for cool climates and offers many of its own introductions. The catalog is highly informative, with an excellent selection of short-season tomatoes.
>Johnny's Selected Seeds
>Albion, Maine 04910

Le Jardin lists unusual varieties of vegetables and herbs.
>Le Jardin du Gourmet
>Box 64
>West Danbury, Vermont 05873

Nichols sells herbs and gourmet vegetables, including the true saffron crocus and the luffa sponge gourd.
>Nichols Garden Nursery
>1190 North Pacific Highway
>Albany, Oregon 97321

Plants of the Southwest offers crops native to or adapted to the Southwest. as well as drought-tolerant ornamental trees and shrubs and Southwestern wildflowers. Also, special seed mixtures for drought-hardy lawns.
>Plants of the Southwest
>1570 Pacheco Street
>Santa Fe, New Mexico 87501

Park's lists a good selection of Oriental vegetables. Despite its southern location, Park's offers early varieties, too.
>George W. Park Seed Co., Inc.
>Greenwood, South Carolina 29647

Stark's doesn't sell seeds but offers an excellent selection of fruit trees, grapes and berries. This is some of the finest stock that can be purchased in the United States.
>Stark Brother's Nurseries
>Louisiana, Missouri 63353

Thompson and Morgan has a complete listing of vegetables, including many that are unavailable from other catalogs.

Thompson and Morgan, Inc.
P.O. Box 531
Pittston, Pennsylvania 18640

This company offers hard-to-find and old-fashioned, or heirloom varieties.
Vermont Bean Seed Company
49 Garden Lane
Bomoseen, Vermont 05732

There are numerous small seed companies scattered throughout the country. Check in your area for any local seed companies. Usually they'll be selling vegetable varieties that do well in your area. Other small, specialized companies offer seed that can't be found in the larger catalogs. The best way to locate these companies is in the classified ads of gardening magazines and local periodicals.

Bugs are an unavoidable part of the gardening experience and once they are understood, they become easier to deal with. The high desert gardener doesn't have as many kinds of insect pests to contend with as gardeners in wetter areas do, so in that sense, high desert gardening is actually easier.

The best medicine for garden pests it that proverbial ounce of prevention. Always keep in mind that the less hospitable the environment, the less likely are heavy pest infestations. For instance, many insects like to hide and breed under boards, boxes and plant remains. By keeping the garden free of debris, bugs are forced to look elsewhere for their breeding grounds and living quarters.

Plant remains should be promptly removed to the compost heap or they should be tilled into the soil. If the plants were diseased, the remains should be burned well away from the garden or hauled to the dump. Weeds and grasses around the perimeter of the garden should be kept low. If a rototiller is available, the perimeter can be tilled in the spring and fall to expose eggs and larvae.

Another preventative measure is tilling. Turning the soil over in the late fall, after the majority of the crops have been harvested, will expose the eggs of many garden pests to the elements and to predators. Fall tilling is especially effective in controlling grasshoppers, cutworms, corn earworms and, to some extent, squash bugs. Areas of the garden that have wintered-over vegetables such as carrots can be turned over in late winter or early spring, after the harvest. This still leaves time for the weather and the birds (especially the birds) to go to work on any eggs or larvae that might be lurking in the soil.

Crop rotation is as effective in reducing pest infestations as it is in reducing the incidence of plant disease. Growing the same crop in the same place year after year encourages the pests specific to that crop to stick around for the annual feast. By rotating the crop, you eliminate the immediately available food source that newly hatched pests need, thus reducing the pest population.

Finally, an effective way to avoid harmful insect infestations is to avoid the use of pesticides. Pesticides don't only kill the pests; they can kill predatory insects, earthworms and birds, and they can seriously upset the delicate ecological balance of the high desert. Once this ecological balance is upset, even if it is only the ecosystem of a city block, pest infestations become more likely and more difficult to control. Thus the use of harsh chemical pesticides can begin a vicious circle of creating imbalances that lead to more severe pest problems that lead to a need to use more pesticides. And if that isn't bad enough, most chemical pesticides are dangerous to handle and use, and some even have been shown to cause birth defects.

As the dangers of chemical pesticides became a real concern in the United States, many researchers turned to the animal world for ways to control insects. What they found was that nature has provided numerous insects that feed on other insects. Lucky for the high desert gardener that many of these beneficial insects occur naturally in the high desert.

The best known beneficial insect is probably the ladybug. This charming little creature can be found crawling on most plants in search of aphids. Its larvae, which aren't as pretty or as obvious as the ladybug itself, also have a definite taste for aphids. Ladybugs usually show up in the garden all by themselves but if they are scarce in your garden, ladybugs can be purchased by the pint! Remember though, if there isn't enough food for the ladybugs they will fly off to buggier pastures.

Another beneficial insect that most people are familiar with is the praying mantis. This large and rather formidable insect is not as common in

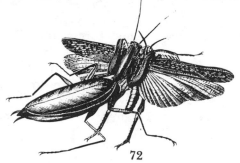

72

the high desert as it is in the wetter climates. The mantis seems to occur naturally in the high desert only around damp areas such as lakes, rivers, streams and marshes. Mantids can be purchased and introduced into the garden. Keep in mind that they, too, will head for greener pastures if there isn't enough food to eat. Also, mantids are not discriminating eaters and will consume some beneficials along with the pests.

Very common in the high desert is the lovely little lacewing. It is either brown or green, depending on how close you are to the Rockies and which side you are on. The brown is the Western lacewing, but here in Santa Fe I have seen the green Eastern lacewing too. Named for its finely veined, translucent wings, the lacewing likes to hang out in the garden for its meal of aphids and mealybugs. The larvae are not as selective and they will consume mites, scales, thrips, leafhopper nymphs and caterpillar eggs.

Strange as it may seem, the fly family provides a number of very helpful predators. The robber fly resembles a cross between a fly and a wasp, and it looks quite threatening but is completely harmless to people. It does harm moths and butterflies and their larvae, and it also eats beetles and grasshoppers. The robber fly's larvae eat grubs and grasshopper eggs. They like to live under mulch and enjoy an environment that has decaying organic matter, so they should be right at home in any well-cared for soil.

The hover fly is frequently mistaken for a tiny bee or wasp, and it is found buzzing around flowers. It feeds on pollen and nectar, but its larvae eat leafhoppers, aphids and mealybugs. The larvae aren't pretty, resembling a cross between a maggot and a slug, so be careful not to mistake them for some awful pest.

Tachinid flies look just like houseflies but they provide a useful service to the gardener instead of being the general nuisance that houseflies are. These flies are parasites and lay their eggs in the bodies of caterpillars. The eggs hatch and the larvae feed on the host from the inside out. This is certainly a dreadful image but one has to admit that it's rather ingenious. Some tachinids parasitize Mexican bean beetles.

The Calosoma beetle, known far and wide as the stinkbug, is a common sight in the high desert. This beetle is large, growing up to one and one-half inches in length, and has a shiny black body. When disturbed it will raise its back end in the air and let off a very disagreeable odor. The Calosoma eats large amounts of caterpillars and other insect pests and should be allowed to go about its business undisturbed, stinky or not.

There are a number of other beetles that are helpful in the garden. There are a few that I've found in my garden but have never been able to positively identify. After close observation, I learned that they weren't doing any damage to the plants, so I assumed that they were either beneficial or neutral garden residents.

Although spiders aren't insects (they're arachnids), they are beneficial garden residents. Spiders have been the recipients of a very bad rap since only one spider common to the high desert — the black widow — is a real threat to humans. Luckily, this beautiful but dangerous spider is not commonly found in the garden. Sure, other spiders may bite, but the bite is usually painless and rarely raises a lump larger than a mosquito bite.

Many kinds of spiders normally inhabit the vegetable garden. Some build orb webs, others build haphazard webs and still others live under mulch, building no web at all.

The most striking of the web-building spiders is the common garden spider, a large, yellow-and-black spider who builds a large, perfect orb web. The garden spider is beautiful to see early in the morning, sitting the in the middle of its web, with moisture clinging to the delicate strands. Most other spiders are less spectacular than the common garden spider, except the tarantula, but they are all just as helpful.

Spiders eat live insects that happen to jump, fall or land in their webs. Spiders that don't build webs, such as the wolf spiders, chase their prey. In all cases, except that of the black widow, the gardener's policy on spiders must be to accept them as unappealing allies and never to kill them.

When most of us think of wasps, we picture the large, thin-bodied types that build large nests and inflict painful stings. Many wasps, however, are tiny and harmless and perform a useful service for the gardener and orchardist.

The Braconid wasp is among the most helpful of the parasitic wasps. It lays its eggs in the bodies of numerous caterpillars and beetles. The larvae eat the host and then pupate on the host or nearby insects. The tomato hornworm is often found with tiny white cocoons attached to its back; these are the pupating braconid wasps. Instead of letting it munch away on her tomatoes, the wise gardener will catch the hornworm, and confine it until the wasps hatch.

Of the Chalcid wasps, the trichogramma is the best known to the organic gardener. This tiny wasp parasitizes aphids, scales, mealybugs and the larve of many beetles, butterflies and moths. The trichogramma can be purchased from mail-order garden supply houses and released into the garden. The trichogramma is also helpful in the orchard.

There are other, non-insect garden residents that are very helpful. A very common beneficial animal is the lizard. In mid-spring, lizards will start showing up in the garden, looking for water and bugs. They will remain in and around the garden until the weather turns cold in the fall. If lizards don't show up on their own, even though there are plenty of bugs in the garden, they can be imported. Lizard-catching is an excellent chore for children.

While lizards are common throughout the high desert, toads tend to show up in lesser numbers. They are more common around the wetter areas of the high desert and they seem to spontaneously generate after the first good rain of the summer. Toads eat lots of insects. In fact, it is estimated that a single toad will eat up to 15,000 insects in a single season!

The snake is another high desert creature who's gotten a lot of bad press. Rattlesnakes are the only high desert snakes that pose a threat to people, yet they are shy creatures, preferring to live well away from people and to hide themselves when humans approach. Bull snakes, on the other hand, seem to like living among people and in return for your tolerance they will eat gophers and mice. It is interesting to note that when a bull snake feels threatened, it will coil and hiss like a rattlesnake without the rattle.

Birds are much more of a help than a hindrance in the garden. Though ravens and crows are abundant, they rarely bother the garden, especially if dogs are in the neighborhood. Some of the most helpful birds are the western meadowlark, all flycatchers, the American kestrel (sparrow hawk), the loggerhead shrike, the Northern oriole, the Western kingbird, the mourning dove, the Western tanager, the barn swallow, all woodpeckers, the house finch and the mountain bluebird. Some birds are a mixed bag, especially birds of prey such as owls and hawks, because they eat snakes and lizards. The migratory Brewers blackbird eats insects but tends to disturb the garden a bit. My gardens have never suffered serious damage from foraging birds.

All beneficial animals, be they snakes, spiders, wasps or birds, are very susceptible to the hazards of pesticides. In areas where pesticides have been used intensely, such as some of the national forests and the ranges infested with grasshoppers, beneficial animals and insects may be in very short supply. It is in everyone's interest to reintroduce as many beneficials as is possible. It is also in everyone's interest to lobby hard against massive applications of harmful pesticides.

While beneficials go a long way in insect pest control, they don't always prevent serious infestations. In the past 10 years, researchers have discovered numerous microbial pathogens that safely control some insect pests without upsetting the balance of the food chain. Two of these microbial controls are currently available to home gardeners and are perfectly safe to use. It is reasonable to expect more and more microbial controls to be approved by the Environmental Protection Agency (EPA) and made available to gardeners.

Bacillus thuringiensis (BT) is a pathogen that infects the larvae of most butterflies and moths. It is sprayed or dusted on the affected plants and when ingested by the caterpillar, it paralyzes its digestive tract and kills it. Simple as that. BT is highly effective against tent caterpillars, tomato hornworms, cabbage loopers and the imported cabbage worm, but it is effective on just about any other caterpillar. BT is applied only when an infestation occurs, and is safe for birds, lizards and other predators to ingest.

Nosema locustae is a microscopic organism that infects grasshoppers but does not reduce the hopper population immediately. The grasshopper must ingest bait with Nosema locustae. Then it takes 21 days for the pathogen to establish itself in the hopper. An infected grasshopper eventually turns a sickly yellow, becomes sluggish and stops feeding. Infected females pass the disease on to their progeny.

The best way to apply Nosema locustae, commony called grasshopper spore, is to place the bait throughout the garden and the yard, especially where grasshoppers are the most numerous. In a small neighborhood, the spore is most effective if other residents apply it in their yards. In rural areas, grasshopper spore should be spread in all parts of the property, especially weed patches.

Grasshopper spore is most effective one or two years after the first application. Since rural areas, especially range areas, are prone to migrating hoppers, the spore should be applied once a year for two or three years in an effort to infect a large percentage of the migrating population.

Recently a safe pesticide was approved by the EPA and the FDA for use on flowers and vegetables. Insecticidal soap is a concentrate of the property in soap that kills certain pests. Insecticidal soap is very effective on aphids, thrips, white flies and some scales. This pesticide breaks down into simple forms and does not remain in the food chain.

Pyrethrum is another pesticide that breaks down into simple forms and doesn't stay in the food chain. It is a potent pesticide that kills insect pests and beneficials, too. Rotenone comes in this category also. When using these two organic, biodegradable pesticides, follow instructions carefully. I try to save these pesticides for severe cases that just won't respond to milder treatments. Also keep in mind that rotenone and pyrethrum aren't effective on all pests.

## COMMON HIGH DESERT GARDEN PESTS
## AND THEIR CONTROL

**Ants** – The large black or red ants that have a painful bite are frequently found in gardens but they don't do serious damage. In general, they tend to be scavengers. Some ants, usually small black ones, tend aphids for their sweet "milk" — a substance the aphids exude. The best way to solve this problem is to control the aphids.

Tiny, soft-body black ants may cause problems. One summer they attacked the leaf axils on my potato plants. Trying to figure out how to control them, I remembered that we used to call them sugar ants because they went for drops of honey and fruit juice when they got inside the house. So I put out a trap: a shallow jar lid filled with honey. I placed the jar lid so its lip was even with the soil surface. Within an hour, the ants had swarmed around the trap. Many of them fell in and died in the sticky trap, while others carried food off to the nest. Although it didn't get rid of the nest, the trap diverted the ants' attention from the potatoes.

**Aphids** – Sometimes called plant lice, aphids can be serious pests. They suck the juices out of leaves, stems and buds and they also spread disease. If ladybugs and lacewings aren't controlling the aphid population, you may want to import more ladybugs. Or trap the aphids with yellow strips covered with a sticky substance. The aphids are attracted to the yellow color and are then caught by the sticky stuff. These strips can be made or they can be purchased. Insecticidal soap is very effective against aphids.

**Asparagus Beetle** – This colorful pest is sometimes a problem in the high desert. The best way to avoid infestations is to shallowly cultivate around the plants in the fall. This exposes the beetle larvae to the elements and predators. Planting tomatoes near asparagus helps to discourage the bug, as do nasturtiums and calendula (pot marigold). If things get really out of hand, rotenone will control the beetles and their grubs.

**Beet Leafhopper** – The leafhopper is one-eighth of an inch long, yellow-green in color and very nimble. It comes in from fields and weed patches and does its damage by spreading curly top, a debilitating disease that affects beans, beets, lettuce, spinach, squash and, most of all, tomatoes. Since the leafhopper breeds in garden trash and weeds, garden sanitation is the most effective way to prevent infestations. Keep weeds low around the garden perimeters and keep the garden itself well-weeded.

**Blister Beetle** – There are many types of blister beetles. The ones that do the damage in the high desert are slender and grayish in color. They usually come in swarms and devour most anything, though they seem to prefer tomatoes, potatoes, beets, chard and squash. They are supposed to exude a substance that causes blisters; they have never had that effect on the hands of the many gardeners I've spoken to. Luckily, blister beetles don't stick around all season. In small swarms, they can be controlled by hand picking. Use gloves if they cause blisters. If there are too many to control by hand picking, sabadilla dust, a safe pesticide made from the seeds of the sabadilla plant, a tropical member of the lily family, may be used. Handle with caution as the dust can irritate mucous membranes.

**Cabbage Looper** – This inch-worm that ranges from green to muddy brown in color is a pest of the entire cabbage family. It isn't a serious pest in the high desert and it is easy to control. Handpick any that you find and then spray the affected crop with BT. Remember that it is useless to spray BT until the pest appears.

**Colorado Potato Beetle** – This pest can seriously damage potato crops. It is round, about three-eighths of an inch in length with black-and-yellow stripes running the length of the wings. Garlic, marigolds and beans are effective potato beetle repellants. Plant them among the potatoes and there should be no major infestations. The best way to control beetles that do appear is to handpick them and kill them. Ladybugs also control this pest.

**Corn Earworm** – This ugly larva of an equally ugly moth becomes even uglier when you see what it does to your corn. The earworm can be a major vegetable garden pest. Eggs are laid in the newly emerging silk and the larvae start by feeding on the silk and then burrowing into the ear where they feed on the kernels. What a disappointment to husk and ear of corn and find one third of the ear devoured by the ugly worm!

The corn earworm is difficult to control. Early varieties of corn suffer less damage than the late-ripening varieties. Resistant varieties with very tight husks can be grown.

BT has been found to affect the earworm. The dust or spray can be applied to the silk to get the worms while they're young. I've found that this reduces their population by about 50 percent. A BT solution can also be dropped into the developing ear with an eyedropper. Hopefully, the earworm will consume it and die. BT will not prevent pollination and washes off in the rain.

Earworms can also be handpicked before they enter the ear itself. As soon as the ears "silk out," begin checking the silk for worms. They will be very small. Damaged silk, with a sawdustlike substance on it, is a sure sign of earworms. Both BT applications and handpicking are time consuming but I've found them to be very inexpensive and well worth full ears of sweet and succulent corn.

Pyrethrum, if it can make contact with the earworms, is also effective. Keep in mind that it also kills beneficials such as the trichogramma wasp, which is said to be somewhat effective against the earworm.

**Crickets** – If you discover crickets in the garden, leave them be; they don't seem to do much damage to anything. If you do find that they are doing damage, the only way to control them is by handpicking, which is difficult. Tilling in the fall and keeping weeds to a miniumum are the best ways to avoid large cricket infestations.

**Cucumber Beetles** – The spotted cucumber beetle often shows up in high desert gardens. This pest feeds on squash, melons, cucumbers, tomatoes, cabbage, asparagus and beets. Usually its numbers aren't enough to do serious harm, but occasionally large and damaging infestations may occur. I have successfully chased them away with dustings of ground cayenne pepper. Also try insecticidal soap, and as a last resort, rotenone. Tilling in the fall and crop rotation are effective ways to avoid serious infestations.

**Cutworms** – The cutworm is a serious pest in the spring garden. This voracious larva of a brown moth hatches in early spring and particularly likes to chew on spinach and lettuce seedlings. Later on in the season, the cutworm will eat most any young and tender vegetable. I've found them on the usually invincible onion. By mid-to-late May, the cutworm is gone.

Cutworms come in all colors, from green to khaki to dark brown. They feed at night. Some chew the stems flush with the soil surface while others climb the stems and consume the leaves. Cutworm collars, described in the section on transplanting, protect seedlings from the surface feeders, but other types climb right over the collar and up the plant. The tiny seedlings of spinach, lettuce, radishes and onions are indefensible against the worms. The best strategy is to go out every evening around 10 o'clock or so with a powerful flashlight. Pick the cutworms off the plants and squash them under a well-placed foot. This nightly vigil must be kept up thoughout April and well into May.

To prevent infestations, or to at least decrease the population, till the soil deeply in the fall. Areas that will be planted in the early spring should be tilled again a couple of weeks before planting, although it is now recommended that the entire garden be tilled in late winter to expose the larvae and destroy the tiny blades of grass and weeds that are the larvae's first foods. If you find seedlings that have been chewed or cut at the base, gently scrape the soil around the seedling. Usually a cutworm will be hiding just below the surface.

**Earwigs** – The ugly earwig is another night feeder and is an infrequent but destructive pest. The best way to control earwigs is to trap them. Loosely crumple some newspaper into a small flower pot. Set the pot upside down on a small stick so it doesn't quite touch the ground. In the morning you can drop the sleeping earwigs into a jar filled with some toxic substance like bleach, ammonia or turpentine.

**Flea Beetles** – This tiny black beetle is aptly named because it is a very nimble jumper. It feeds on most any plant but prefers members of the cabbage family, eggplant and nasturtiums. To protect these plants as seedlings, when the flea beetles can be the most harmful, sprinkle them with wood ashes. When the plants are bigger, the flea beetles will give their leaves a shot-hole look but rarely do serious damage. At this point they can be controlled with a spray of a garlic or onion infusion. Put lots of garlic cloves in two cups of water, blend it and let it sit overnight. The next day strain out the little pieces and spray the affected plants. In the worst infestations, rotenone will work.

Good garden sanitation is the most effective way to prevent infestations. Till the soil in the fall, remove plant residues promptly and control weeds.

**Grasshoppers** – These guys can be hand-picked or grasshopper spore (nosema locustae) can be applied for a more permanent control. (See the discussion of grasshopper spore earlier in this chapter.) Tilling in the fall exposes hopper eggs to the weather and to predators. Blister beetle larvae eat grasshopper larvae.

**Harlequin Bugs** – This bug is one of the shield bugs, so named for the shape of their bodies. The harlequin bug is very pretty but in large numbers it can do serious damage to the cabbage family, corn, lettuce, beans, potatoes and asparagus. I have always found a few harlequin bugs in my garden and hand-picking is the best control. Also look for their distinctive eggs on the underside of leaves. They look like tiny white barrels with black stripes lined up in two neat rows. Destroy any eggs you find. Pyrethrum or rotenone can be used in the case of a big infestation.

**June Beetles** – Also called a May beetle, this hard-shelled flying beetle is rarely a major garden pest. It's ugly, whitish-gray grub will sometimes feed on the roots of corn and potatoes. Birds do a good job of keeping this pest in check. While working in the garden, destroy the grubs as you find them.

**Leaf Miners** – These tiny caterpillars and maggots are a frequent high desert pest that tunnel in the leaves of Swiss chard and spinach, making the leaf inedible. They used to be difficult to control but are now easily trapped with yellow stick strips that can be made at home or purchased.

**Mexican Bean Beetle** – This voracious pest is the black sheep of the ladybug family. Potatoes repel the bean beetle and beans repel the potato beetle making them excellent companion plants. Small infestations are easily controlled by hand-picking the round, dull, copper-colored beetles. The Mexican bean beetle is not a serious pest in the high desert, despite our proximity to Mexico.

**Rodents** – Rabbits, mice and gophers can all be troublesome pests in the home garden. Rabbits are easily fenced out with special rabbit fencing or with small-hole chicken wire. To fence out gophers, the fencing has to be buried at least six inches into the soil and sometimes that doesn't work. Daffodils repel gophers but a garden border requires a lot of water. Gopher spurge, another gopher repellant, also uses a lot of water and is toxic to people. Dumping used kitty litter down gopher holes will drive them away in a hurry (but don't use the kitty litter in the garden). The presence of dogs seems to deter the gophers and cats often hunt them. Flooding the holes will sometimes drive them out. If worse comes to worse, poisoned bait can be put in the holes that are outside the garden. Some people recommend trapping the gophers live, but it is very hard to coax a gopher out of its hole.

If mice are bothering the garden, set out traps baited with cheese. That should work very quickly. Snakes, hawks and kestrels are great rodent controllers. Kestrels can be attracted to the back yard with a special house (see Plants of the Southwest's catalog).

**Sap Beetles** – These black beetles are little more than an eighth of an inch long. They feed on corn ears by making little round holes in the husk or by entering through the silk. I find that pyrethrum controls them.

**Squash Bugs** – This black shield bug can be a major headache for high desert gardeners, although it seems that some areas have it and some don't. The squash bug sucks the juices out of the leaves and stems of all members of the Cucurbitaceae family: summer and winter squash, pumpkins, cucumbers and melons. When disturbed, the squash bug lets off a very unpleasant odor.

The squash bug is difficult to control. The most effective method is hand-picking them, especially in the beginning of the season when the population is manageable. If the population can be kept small until mid-August, affected plants will usually be able to healthily survive the rest of the season, but don't give up picking them. Look for squash bugs under the leaves during the heat of the day or on top of the leaves in the cool morning hours. Eggs are a reddish-brown in color and are laid on the underside of leaves and stems. They are easily crushed. Soft-shelled nymphs are green and later turn gray, and they are easily crushed. The adult is tough and ugly and is best killed by dropping it into a jar of ammonia.

The best prevention is to maintain a clean garden and to till the soil in the fall and again in the spring.

**Squash Vine Borer** – Here is another nasty pest that is very difficult to control. The borer is the larva of an inconspicuous moth that lays her eggs in the stem, close to the base of the plant. The eggs hatch and the larvae penetrate the stem and tunnel through it, eating as they go. Their presence is betrayed by a sawdustlike material that oozes from the base of the vine.

If they are detected early enough, borers can be removed by slitting the vine with a sharp knife. Take out the larvae and destroy them, then bury the vine in damp soil with the hope that it will root. Borers that go undetected will cause the vine and its leaves to suddenly wilt, never to perk up again.

The borer moth shows up to lay her eggs just as the squash plants begin to vine, which is usually late June and early July. One way to prevent the borer infestation is to wait until late June or early July to plant your summer squash. Unfortunately this late planting doesn't provide enough time for most winter squash to mature.

There is some evidence that wrapping the stems of the young vines with pantyhose prevents the moth from laying her eggs. Do this as soon as the plants begin to vine. Rotenone can be be sprinkled at regular intervals as the plants begin to vine in hopes that it will kill the eggs, the moth itself or the newly-hatched larvae. Once again, good garden sanitation and fall and spring tilling are good preventive measures.

**Thrips** – This insect is slender and tiny, about one-sixteenth of an inch long. Thrips feed on most plants but do little damage. They will scar the pods of beans and peas, and I've seen them destroy squash blossoms. A few applications of ground cayenne pepper gets rid of thrips and insecticidal soap is also effective.

**Tomato Hornworm** – This giant-size caterpillar is bright green and blends in remarkably with tomatoes and potatoes, but less so on eggplants and peppers. The hornworm prefers succulent young tomato leaves but it will settle for potatoes, too.

Usually you will stumble across the hornworm while working in the tomato patch. Of course, hand-pick and destroy any that you find. After you have discovered them, treat the tomatoes, potatoes and eggplants with BT. Reapply in a few days and another application one week later should take care of the hornworm problem. If a hornworm is found with tiny white torpedoes on its back, let it remain; it is carrying the pupae of the beneficial braconid wasp.

There is nothing as depressing as discovering a once-flourishing seedling stripped of its leaves or lying toppled over on the ground. An unpleasant apprehension fills the once happy gardener. Most people tend to panic and run off to the store to buy an all-purpose bug spray. They spray the entire garden, beneficial insects and all.

The best defense against garden pests is observation and education. Before trying to control a pest, you have to know what it is and what its habits are. If you intend to do any serious gardening, be sure you have a good reference book on garden pests with clear pictures.

Once damage is discovered, search out the culprit. This may take a couple of seconds or it may take a few minutes sitting still or rummaging through the plants. Look hard; many pests blend right in with their favorite plant. If the pest isn't discovered during the day, a night search will be in order. Once you identify the pest, choices can be made wisely and, in most cases, the use of poisons can be averted.

Remember that there will always be pests in the garden. No garden is perfect; there are always a few chewed leaves or a few lost tomatoes. Plant

enough so that you can afford to give up a few things to the bugs. Think of it as appeasing the gods.

Plant diseases can be very frustrating. Caused by bacterium, viruses and fungi, some diseases can be very difficult to control and almost impossible to stop once they get started. Luckily for the high desert gardener, the dry climate does not promote most plant diseases so there aren't many to contend with.

A plant growing in a well-maintained soil is generally a happy plant and much less subject to disease. Always work to maintain a high level of organic matter and always practice crop rotation.

Good garden sanitation is another important disease prevention measure. Don't let plants sit and rot in the garden. Turn them into the soil or remove them to the compost heap. Remove all diseased plants to the dump or burn them.

Some diseases are transmitted by pests that hop in from neighboring yards and fields. These are the most difficult to control. Aphids and leafhoppers are the main disease-carriers in the high desert. Taking measures to control these two pests is the best defense against insect-borne disease.

A good reference book is necessary to identify diseases. Sometimes the symptoms are so similar it's nearly impossible to decide what kind of wilt a plant has. The county agricultural extension agent can help you identify some of the more puzzling diseases.

Once a diseased plant has been identified, it should be removed from the garden and destroyed. Avoid infecting other plants by washing your hands or gloves before touching other plants. Once you know that a certain disease has shown up in your garden, it is best to plant varieties that are resistant to that disease. There are plenty of disease-resistant vegetables on the market and seed catalogs will list any resistant qualities a plant variety might have.

A final note for tobacco smokers: wash your hands before handling peppers, tomatoes, potatoes and eggplants. All are susceptible to a viral disease called tobacco mosaic. Do not smoke around these plants.

# ORCHARDS IN THE HIGH DESERT XII

Growing fruit trees in the high desert isn't much different than growing them in other parts of the country. All the popular, temperate-climate-fruits — peaches, pears, apples, apricots, cherries and most plums — will grow in the high desert. Apricots, peaches, sweet cherries and plums may be unreliable producers in the higher elevations where late spring frosts are common. If possible, choose varieties of these fruits that are late-blooming. Your county agricultural extension agent can give you a list of recommended varieties for your specific locale.

Since fruit tree culture in the high desert is so similar to their culture elsewhere, this chapter will provide simple tips that will make high desert fruit tree culture more successful. For more specific information, consult a comprehensive book about organic fruit tree culture.

The high desert seems somewhat more susceptible to late spring frosts than other parts of the country. This is especially true of the high mountain valleys. Cool air rolls off the slopes at night and settles in the valley so often the valley will experience a late frost while the slopes above it won't.

To avoid crop loss due to a late frost, the best place to situate an orchard is on a north-facing slope. The slope warms up slowly in the spring and that delays blossoming, hopefully until the weather has settled. That reduces the risk of blossom damage due to a late spring frost. This tactic isn't foolproof but it does decrease the chances of frost damage.

If a north slope isn't available, choose a location that is likely to warm up slowly in the spring. A southern slope, of course, will warm up quickly in the spring and almost always cause fruit trees to bloom early.

If you live in a windy area, you may want to consider a site that is sheltered from the prevailing winds. Avoid the south side of a structure, however, or once again you'll run the risk of early blooming.

Take the soil quality into consideration. A sandy soil doesn't hold water well and that can cause real problems for fruit trees trying to make it in the high desert. Also avoid areas with a shallow layer of caliche. Water will stand and cause roots to rot, or the tree's roots won't be able to penetrate the caliche and the tree will be stunted.

A healthy orchard starts with healthy stock. Be sure to purchase the trees from a reputable nursery, be it mail-order or local.

The best kind of trees to start an orchard with are bare-root trees. These are young trees usually no more than five feet tall, that have been dug from the ground while they're dormant. Their roots have only a little soil clinging to them and they are kept moist in a wrapping of sphagnum peat moss, shredded newpaper and/or plastic bags.

Bare-root stock has many advantages. First of all, there is a wider selection of varieties available bare root. Most potted fruit trees are limited to the most popular varieties which aren't necessarily the best varieties for high desert growing. Dwarf, semi-dwarf and standard-size trees are all available as bare-root stock.

The second advantage is that bare-root trees establish more quickly than potted trees and get off to a better start. They don't have to make a big adjustment going from the high-quality potting soil to the usually lower quality soil of the orchard site. The bare-root tree is planted when it's dormant and as it "wakes up," it sends its roots out into its new environment long before the leaves open. This provides the tree with a good foundation to support healthy and rapid top growth. It is widely agreed that bare-root trees grow faster and better than potted trees and often catch up to the generally larger potted trees in one or two seasons. Trees planted bare-root also tend to bear their first crop earlier than the potted trees.

The biggest trick for successfully planting fruit trees, be they bare-root or potted, is to plant them in a big hole. The general rule is to provide a hole that is twice as wide and twice as deep as the root ball. However, a bigger hole doesn't hurt.

Follow planting instructions that accompany the tree. This is especially important when setting the tree in the hole because most fruit trees are grafted and , depending on the tree, the graft may have to be close to the soil surface or a few inches above it.

When filling the planting hole in, the soil should be modified. Fruit trees seem to put up with the high desert's difficult soils but improving the soil immediately around the newly-planted tree is a way to make sure the tree gets off to a good start. A good soil mix for filling the hole is one part original soil, one part sphagnum peat moss and one part well-rotted manure or compost. Stir in a few very generous handfuls of bone meal.

When filling the hole, be sure that there are no air pockets around the roots. When the hole has been filled half way, water the tree with couple of gallons of mild manure tea or a mild fish emulsion fertilizer and allow the solution to soak in. Then fill in the remainder of the hole, leaving a slight trough around the tree to catch rain. Tamp the soil and water again, using plain old water.

A steady supply of water is essential for a happy and healthy orchard. Drip irrigation was originally designed to water orchards and is by far the best way to irrigate high desert orchards of all sizes. The trees in my young orchard were progressing satisfactorily when I was watering them once or twice a week by filling their troughs with water. After the drip system was installed, the trees made exceptional growth. An added bonus was the time, energy and water the drip system saves. However, I've left the troughs around the tree to help catch rain.

To help conserve the precious water applied to the trees, use a mulch of straw or compost. Keep the mulch a few inches from the trunk of the tree to prevent diseases and discourage insects.

Pruning is one part of orchard maintenance that frightens many people, even experienced gardeners. It is difficult to clip off healthy young branches, even though you know it will be best for the tree in the long run. Numerous pruning guides are available with very extensive instructions, so I won't go into the actual mechanics here. A good way to learn to prune is to have an experienced pruner show you how.

When pruning, remember that you are helping to steer the tree into its healthiest shape. Work with the tree's natural growth habit; don't try to turn it into something it isn't, unless you are trying espalier methods against fences or walls. Those methods are tricky but are excellent for people with limited space.

The best time to prune is in the late winter or early spring, just as the buds are beginning to swell. Most gardeners come to enjoy pruning as they see the results of their careful and prudent clipping.

As in vegetable gardening, the high desert orchardist doesn't have quite as many pests and diseases to handle as do most other orchardists.

In the insect department, the major preventive measure is to keep the orchard free of debris and to keep the grasses clipped. Once again, good sanitation practices help to eliminate the hiding places and nesting spots of many pests.

A main weapon against many insect pests is the annual spring application of dormant oil spray. This spray contains a very high grade of oil. It is applied in late winter or very early spring, just as the buds swell but before they actually begin to open. All parts of the tree are coated with the spray.

Dormant oil spray is very effective against scales, whiteflies, mealybugs, thrips, aphids and codling moths. No one is quite sure exactly why the spray works but it is thought that the oil interferes with gas exchange and more or less suffocates its victims. When purchasing dormant oil spray, be sure that it does not contain Bordeaux mixture, which is really arsenate of lead, a potent poison. Mix the spray according to instructions and apply on a windless day with the temperature above 40 degrees.

Ants can be a problem in the high desert orchard. They like to farm aphids or eat young fruit, depending on the ant. Luckily, they are easily controlled. A number of companies market a sticky substance that can be safely applied to the tree trunk. All climbing insects get stuck on their way up the tree and never make it to the top. On young trees, the sticky stuff is often applied to heavy paper that's been wrapped around the trunk.

Peach, apricot and cherry trees are sometimes plagued by borers. Avoid injuries to the trunk and keep a watchful eye for any sawdust around a hole near the base of the tree. A band of sticky stuff (frequently called by one brand name: Tanglefoot) around the trunk at the base of the tree will foil

the moth when she tries to lay her eggs. Moth balls (napthalene) distributed around the trunk may repel some of the moths.

A number of caterpillars like to eat fruit tree leaves. These include tent caterpillars and leaf rollers. Most caterpillars are easily controlled with Bacills thruingiensis (BT).

Birds just love to eat young fruit (and sometimes blossoms), especially the smaller fruits such as cherries and plums. The only effective way to outsmart these otherwise helpful critters is to purchase and use orchard netting. Cover the trees as soon as the fruit is set, or before blossoming if you have "blossom-eaters."

Thanks to the high desert's usually low humidity, there are very few diseases that affect fruit trees. Fireblight, a bacterial disease, is the only one worth mentioning. Though it is rare, it can be devastating when it hits. Pears are the most susceptible but apples can be affected too.

Prevention of fireblight is difficult. There a few varieites of pears and apples that are resistant to the disease. Also avoid planting pyracantha (firethorn) in your landscape because it harbors the bacteria that cause fireblight.

Be on the alert for chlorosis (see chapter on soil pH). This is indicated by a yellowing of the leaves while the leaf veins remain dark green. If the soil was modified at planting time, chlorosis usually isn't a problem. To keep organic matter content high, well-rotted manure and/or compost can be dug into the soil beneath the tree every year in the early spring. Dig the additions in shallowly, being careful not to disturb the roots.

If chlorosis does occur, a quick-fix solution will be necessary to rescue the tree. Using a root feeder, apply iron directly to the roots of the tree. Special root feeder cartridges designed to alleviate chlorosis are available throughout the high desert. These cartridges can also be used on ornamental trees or shrubs that become chlorotic.

## DROUGHT-TOLERANT PERENNIALS FOR THE HIGH DESERT

Although the following plants are known to tolerate drought, they should be given some extra water during their first season in their new environment. Once they are established, they will be able to stand up to the dry high desert climate. However, some will certainly be improved if they are given some extra water, especially during prolonged dry spells. Many drought tolerant perennials, especially native plants, also tolerate poor soils. Consult your book or nursery about the specific needs of each plant.

| | |
|---|---|
| Achillea - yarrow | Linum - flax; some varieties are annuals |
| Alcea rosa - hollyhock | Oenothera - evening primrose |
| Aquilegia - columbine (best in partial shade) | Papaver orientale - Oriental poppy |
| Artemesia - wormwood | Pennisetum setacum - fountain grass |
| Campsis radicans - trumpet vine | Polygonum aubertii - silverlace vine |
| Coreopsis - some varieties are annuals; check before buying | Rudbeckia hirta - gloriosa daisy |
| Euphorbia myrsinites | Rudbeckia laciniata |
| Gaillardia grandiflora | Santolina |
| Hemerocallis - daylily | Sedum - check specific varieties for cold hardiness |
| Iris, bearded | Verbena rigida |
| Kniphofia uvaria - red-hot poker | Yucca - check specific varieties for cold hardiness |

Don't forget about native wildflowers!

## DROUGHT-TOLERANT SHRUBS FOR THE HIGH DESERT

Even though these shrubs are drought hardy, they should be provided with extra water during their first two seasons so that they become well-established. Deep watering is preferable because it encourages the roots to go deep into the soil, making the shrub even more drought-resistant. Once established, the following shrubs are quite tough in the face of drought. Also, most do not require rich soils. Consult a book or your nursery for the specific needs of each shrub.

Caragana arborescens –
Siberian pea-shrub

Cercocarpus – mountain mahogany;
check for cold hardiness
Chrysothamnus nauseosus – chamisa,
rabbitbrush
Cotinus coggygria – smoke tree

Fallugiia paradoxa – Apache plume;
not alway hardy in coldest areas
Forestiera neomexicana –
New Mexico privet
Juniperus – most varieties tolerate
drought but may require water during
prolonged dry spells
Syringa – lilac

Mahonia – Oregon grape; there are
other varieties but check for cold
hardiness
Potentilla fruticosa – cinquefoil,
potentilla
Quercus gambelii – Gambel oak

Rhus glabra – smooth sumac;
can get to tree-size
Rhus trilobata – sumac;
can get to tree size
Rosa rugosa

Shepherdia arentea – silver buffaloberry

Tamarix – salt cedar; can grow to be
tree-size

## DROUGHT-TOLERANT TREES FOR THE HIGH DESERT

Be sure to supply extra water to these trees so that they can become well-established. Again, deep-watering will promote deep root growth and will help to improve drought tolerance. Use your good judgement to decide when supplemental watering is required. Many drought-tolerant trees will do well in poor soils. Be sure to know the specific needs of the trees you decide to plant.

Catalpa – takes some extra water

Populus – cottonwood; needs regular
watering until it is established

Celtis occidentalis - hackberry; tolerates drought after it is established

Elaeagnus angustifolia - Russian olive; this is a tough tree

Fraxinus velutina - Arizona ash; hardy to -10 degrees F.

Koelreuteria paniculata - goldenrain tree; not always hardy in coldest areas

Pinus edulis - pinon pine

Pinus ponderosa - ponderosa pine; prefers the higher elevations

Ulmus pumila - Chinese elm; very tough and often considered a weed

Populus nigra - Lombardy poplar; grows fast but lives max. of 15 years

Populus tremuloides - quaking aspen; prefers the higher elevations

Robinia pseudoacacia - black locust; real tough

Salix matsudana - hankow willow

Salix matsudana Navajo - Navajo globe willow

Salix matsudana umbraculifera - globe willow

## RECOMMENDED READING
## A BASIC GARDENING BOOKSHELF

Editors of Sunset Books and Sunset Magazine. *Sunset Western Garden Book.* Menlo Park, Ca.: Lane Publishing 1979. This book is not strong on organic gardening but it has an excellent listing of individual plants and their care.

Halpin, Anne, ed: and the Editors of Rodale Press. *The Organic Gardener's Guide to Vegetables and Fruits.* Emmaus, Pa.: Rodale Press, 1976.

Hill, Lewis. *Pruning Simplified.* Emmaus, Pa.: Rodale Press, 1979.

Hirshberg, Gary and Gracy Calvan, eds.: and the New Alchemy Institute Staff. *Gardening for All Seasons.* Andover, Mass. Brick House Publishing Company, 1983.

Jeavons, John. *How to Grow More Vegetables.* Berkeley, Ca.: Ten Speed Press, 1982. This book has caused profound changes in the gardening world. Excellent.

Philbrick, Helen and John Philbrick. *The Bug Book.* Charlotte, Vt.: Garden Way Publishing, 1974.

Riotte, Louise. *Carrots Love Tomatoes.* Charlotte, Vt.: Garden Way Publishing, 1975.

Staff of Organic Gardening Magazine. *The Encyclopedia of Organic Gardening.* Emmaus, Pa.: Rodale Press, 1978.

Yepsen, Robert B., ed. *Organic Plant Protection.* Emmaus, Pa.: Rodale Press, 1982.

## SUPPLEMENTAL READING: INSTRUCTIVE & INFORMATIVE

Baker, H.G. *Plants and Civilization.* Belmont, Ca.: Wadsworth Publishing Co., 1970. Describes how plants have shaped the course of world history.

Bartholomew, Mel. *Square Foot Gardening.* Emmaus, Pa.: Rodale Press, 1981.

Carson, Rachel. *Silent Spring.* Bolton: Houghton-Mifflin, 1962. THE argument against pesticides. A classic and must reading.

Hertzberg, Ruth, et.al. *Putting Food By.* New York: Bantam Books, 1975. How to store your garden harvest.

Minnich, Jerry, Marjorie Hunt and the editors of Organic Gardening Magazine. *The Rodale Guide to Composting.* Emmaus, Pa.: Rodale Press, 1979.

# BIBLIOGRAPHY

Brady, Nyle C. *The Nature and Properties of Soil.* New York: Macmillan, 1974.

Editors of Sunset Books and Sunset Magazine. *Sunset New Western Garden Book.* Menlo Park, Ca.: Lane Publishing Company, 1979.

Halpin, Anne, ed. and the Editors of Rodale Press. *The Organic Gardener's Guide to Vegetables and Fruits.* Emmaus, Pa.: Rodale Press, 1976.

Jeavons, John. *How to Grow More Vegetables.* Berkeley, Ca.: Ten Speed Press, 1982.

Research Department of Johnny's Selected Seeds. *Green Manures — A Mini-Manual.* Albion, Maine: Johnny's Selected Seeds Research Department, 1983.

Riotte, Louise. *Carrots Love Tomatoes.* Charlotte, Vt.: Garden Way Publishing, 1975.

Yepsen, Roger B., ed. *Organic Plant Protection.* Emmaus, Pa.: Rodale Press, 1976.

# INDEX

Wasps: 74
Water and watering: 11, 35-38, 52-54
89-90
SEE Also Irrigation
Watermelon: 68
Wind: 10, 17, 39, 85